THE LIFE LEDGER

How to Build a System to Reach Your Goals

JD FROST

FOREWORD BY **TIM STOREY**

SAVIO
REPVBLIC

A SAVIO REPUBLIC BOOK
An Imprint of Post Hill Press
ISBN: 978-1-63758-389-0
ISBN (eBook): 978-1-63758-390-6

The Life Ledger:
How to Build a System to Reach Your Goals
© 2022 by JD Frost
All Rights Reserved

posthillpress.com
New York • Nashville
Published in the United States of America

2 3 4 5 6 7 8 9 10

For my children:

Laney, Sally, and Molly

TABLE OF CONTENTS

FOREWORD

By Tim Storey

There's a difference between wanting to build a better life and actually having a guide like The Life Ledger to show you how to make it happen.

EVERY ONCE IN A WHILE I come across someone who makes me stop and pay attention. After traveling to more than seventy-five countries of the world, you get to meet a wide range of people. When I first met JD Frost, I instantly knew he was a unique man with unique gifts. I have seen firsthand his resiliency in not only his business life, but his personal life as well. I found his understanding of leadership to be at a top level. Not only did he study great leaders and how they led, but he was leading people himself with great results. In this new book, he moves the curtain and shares some of the principles, procedures, the pain, and the price of great leadership.

When I say that his understanding of leadership is top level, I want you to know what I mean. You don't find many accounting firms that are founded by someone who holds an MBA and is also a CPA, but JD does. He used both skillsets to launch Croft & Frost, a successful accounting firm that knows what it takes to start a profitable business. And he leads others on that journey as well. He doesn't just say he's going to show you what to do, he actually gives you step-by-step instruction with tools to implement. You are getting guidance from someone who has led not only his team, but others in a way that you haven't seen before. Great leaders have seen time and time again that talk is cheap. This book goes way beyond talking and shows you how to actually change your life through accountability.

The past decade shows us that there is no shortage of people who study great leaders and how they lead, but I'm noticing that not everyone who studies leaders actually steps into the leader role with great results. It is a unique gift to combine knowledge with specific and measurable action steps that *actually* move the needle in your life. With his firm, he has seen firsthand the inside of some of the most successful companies and knows what it takes to start, lead, and make them grow. He also has seen what causes them to fail. His unique combination of his business background and accounting principles help him to lead others to reach their goals.

The curtains are pulled all the way back as JD shares some of the principles and procedures of great leadership. Getting an insider's view on how JD created not only one, but thirty business ventures is a great opportunity for you. He takes the principles of a business ledger and shows you how to put them into a life ledger in a new and exciting way. Don't you think it's time to start leading your life so you can reach your goals? Not only will you learn what the four foundations of wealth creation are, but you'll learn exactly how to get (and keep) them. You'll learn the pain and price of great leadership from someone who has done it firsthand. I found that when people are willing to share how they have helped clients and investors raise money to get their businesses going, you better pay attention. JD does just that in *The Life Ledger*.

CHAPTER 1

Why You Need to Stop Operating

IF YOU'RE READING THESE WORDS, chances are you feel a little stuck in your life. It might even be that you feel *really* stuck. But the good news is that big or small, being stuck typically starts in the same place—you.

If you haven't already shut the book because you're insulted that I said you're the cause of your own stuckness, great! You're now one step closer to getting *un*stuck and achieving what you've always wanted. Because here's the thing: since you're the one who got yourself into this place, you're also the one who can get yourself out of it. The power to change is yours.

In my experience, both personally and profession-ally, it's not that people aren't trying. It's not that they aren't working hard or trying to do the right thing. They are. It's just that they're going about it in the wrong way. To be more precise, they're operating in the wrong way—because all they're doing is operating.

What do I mean by *operating*? Operating is the time and energy you expend to get things done in your day. Operating is basically how we survive on a daily basis. If you're like me, I've always had this baseline fear of everything going wrong, that somehow it would all come apart. And so for years, I did everything I could to keep my business running on all cylinders—because of the fear that it would fail. I took every call, I tried to charm every client, I tried to fix every problem. I tried to do everything, all the time, every day.

But the thing is, operating might work well enough for surviving, but it's not at all conducive to thriv-ing. When we're simply trying to survive, we can't really thrive—because there's no time left in the day for anything else. You've expended all your time, all your energy, all your headspace on simply trying to stay afloat each day, so there's nothing left. Not only is that shortsighted, it's exhausting. This is how burn-out happens. This is how people get dejected, deflated, depressed. This is how people get stuck.

Operating is also fueled by an underlying feeling of desperation. When I was trying to control every aspect of my business, I wasn't doing it because I thought it was the best way to grow the company, I was doing it because I was desperate to keep it alive. But when we're desperate, when we're always in hyper operating mode, we get tunnel vision. We get set in our ways, and we lose the ability to think differently, think creatively—in some cases, we lose the ability to think at all.

Here's a quick example of what I mean.

A while back, my friend and I bought a piece of property to build an apartment complex. When we first bought the property, we thought it would be a good idea to drive my buddy's truck out to the actual lot—which was out in the middle of nowhere.

We're all amped up and excited to check out the lot. We jump in the truck and drive out across this vast, empty field in the middle of nowhere. We get out and survey the area, which took all of a few minutes because nothing was there—it was literally just an empty field. Then we get back in the truck, put it in drive, and…go absolutely nowhere. We were literally stuck.

I'd like to say we didn't panic—but I can't. We totally did. We were like, holy shit! What the hell are we going to do? We went straight into desperate operating mode. We tried the same things over and over again, developing two main strategies:

⚵ Strategy 1: I got out and pushed while he slammed on the accelerator.

⚵ Strategy 2: He got out and pushed while I slammed on the accelerator.

Guess what? Every time we implemented our strategy, we made the hole deeper. We got more stuck. Yet we kept doing the same thing over and over again. It didn't make any sense. We could see we were digging ourselves into a bigger hole, but it didn't matter because we were working to fix the problem, we were trying our hardest, and we were conditioned to believe that working hard will always just magically solve the problem. It didn't.

And this is what business owners do a lot when they get stuck in the operations of business. They keep thinking, "Well, maybe I'll work a little bit harder. Maybe I'll hire all the right people. Maybe I'll get the best product that doesn't require so much of my time. Maybe I'll start to scale my time even more." That's the same old stuff that doesn't work to grow and scale your business.

You're going to stay stuck, like we were out in the field, until you get out of the car and say, "Hey, I need a towing service to come over here, pull that long line all the way across the field, hook it up to the car, and pull me out of here." That requires other people. It requires other equipment. It requires other expertise. Expertise that you don't have.

Most people don't have the expertise as business owners to grow and scale the business. You have to get other people around you. But that's what keeps business owners getting stuck. They won't take the time to sit back and spend two, three years moving their business in another direction.

And let's be clear, it's scary bringing in other people and giving them responsibility—because they're not you! You, as a business owner, know all the skills, know how to do all those different activities, know every part of the business, you're the expert of your own business as it exists. So when you're the expert, it's really hard to say, "Look, I'll give this to non-experts to do." But this is a necessary step, and it requires getting out of operating mode to see it.

Ultimately, when you're in operating mode, you're living a reactive life, not a proactive one. You don't have a strong grasp of how you're spending your time or what you actually want to accomplish long term because you have no time to do so. What are your plans? What are your goals? What are you actually doing to reach them? Where do you even start?

This is where *The Life Ledger* comes in. I know because it's the way I changed my own life, the way I got out of the hole I had dug myself into.

I am a recovering alcoholic. I can say that now and admit I have a problem and that I needed, and still need, other people's help and support. But for the longest time, I couldn't—partly because I was operating in a way that had brought me some success, or at least what I was considering success at the time. I was a CPA with my own business with forty-eight employees. I was married to a great wife (Lindsey) with three amazing daughters: Laney, Sally, and Molly. I was recognized in my Chattanooga community. From the outside, it looked in many ways like I had it all. But I didn't. I was drinking too much, denying I had a problem, working myself to the bone every day trying to make sure I kept it all together, making sure that I was able to survive another day.

It takes me a long time to learn lessons. I'm a little bit of a slow learner, and I'm not really going to change until my back's up against the wall. With drinking, I kept telling myself it was something I could control. And I tried everything to handle it on my own. I told myself I would only drink beer. I would only drink wine. I would only drink this or I would only drink that. I would only drink on Thursdays or whatever it was. I mean, I was just fooling myself.

At the same time, things started slipping in my marriage, family life, and with my business. The things I had been doing that had worked before weren't working anymore. But I still didn't see it. I couldn't change. I was stuck in operating mode, just trying to control everything in the same way, doing the same things, even though it was clear that I was losing control of everything. I began drinking more, not less. My partner and I split, eventually. My business was starting to fall apart. I was losing clients. Banks were calling me for payments on loans. My employees dwindled from forty-eight to eight. I hit rock bottom in 2019. My greatest fear of everything falling apart was coming true, and it seemed like there was nothing I could do to stop it. I was at an all-time low. I was at a place where I didn't know where else to turn.

And that was it. That was the moment. I think that in order to build conviction, to change your life, you have to get to a place where you have no other decision other than to change. You've got to get to that place where you reach a low or some other catastrophic event happens in your life to where you're like, "This has got to change. This has got to be different." That's when I recalled inspirational speaker and life coach Grant Cardone talking about writing down your goals every day. I never really believed he did it, but I was like, that's what I'm going to do. My first step is going to be to write down my goals twice a day, every day, no matter what.

And from then on, every single day, I have written down my goals. I haven't missed a day. At first it was almost a distraction from all the turmoil going on in my life and all the problems I had. But I knew if I did it, if I just did this one thing, I could accomplish anything if I stayed consistent. And what happened is, over the next several months, everything started changing significantly. And I believe that a lot of that came from writing down my goals twice a day. It's how I ended up building conviction, which is what you need to change your life. Building conviction has to start somewhere, when there's no other decision that you can make other than that one decision. That one decision, for me, began with writing down my goals twice a day and has grown from there.

The Life Ledger is a set of activities and behaviors that you're going to perform over and over and over again, every single day. Writing down your targets, writing down what you're grateful for, writing down your goals twice a day, writing down what will make today great, that's the Life Ledger. The Life Ledger is your practice of discipline on a daily basis that is going to eventually change your behaviors and your life.

The Life Ledger is what you need to rise above the day-to-day grind and really start making it rain. You will never be truly successful until you get yourself out from under the pile of to-do lists, missed messages, and menial tasks. You need to stop doing *everything* and instead start doing what *you are passionate about*. And it works for everyone: business owners, people down on their luck, parents taking care of children, couples working through relationship problems—anyone who wants to enact real change in their life in a way that helps them achieve their goals and make them truly happy.

One of my most fond success stories was also one of my first. I was at an event to help raise money for United Way in my hometown of Chattanooga. One of the speakers talked about "two Chattanoogas": one that is relatively affluent and well off and the other that is struggling in the shadows. The speech inspired me. I knew then that I had to get involved in helping the people who needed help the most. I began listing "helping others get on their feet" in my own Life Ledger, knowing that if I wrote it down as part of my daily process, I would make it happen.

Soon after the event, I met a man named Tony through the United Way. Tony had a hard life and not a lot of opportunity. He had been involved in a gang and spent more than eighteen years in jail. But Tony is a go-getter. He is smart. And he soaks up anything you teach him like a sponge. I liked him the minute I shook his hand.

When we first started meeting, Tony wanted to start a trash collecting business. Unfortunately, he needed to buy a truck before he could do anything, an $80,000 investment. Together, we went over his business plan carefully, and I told them that this idea was not viable. He needed to get some cash in his hands, not get into more debt. I pitched office cleaning. I knew there weren't a lot of high-quality, personable people in the area, and there was a solid opportunity to make his mark in that niche industry.

When he first began his business, I was Tony's only client. He did excellent work, but it was soon obvious to me that he was just going through the motions. He didn't have any *intention* behind his actions. He was saying yes to everything, even if it didn't make sense. Someone would ask him to power-wash their buildings, and he would say yes. Someone else would ask him to do another odd job, and he would say yes. He was clearly in operating mode, just trying to survive.

Ultimately, it wasn't working for him. He wasn't happy, and he was beginning to have doubts about the very idea of owning his own business. I saw his fear and hesitation, and I knew we had to nip it in the bud. I sat him down and started him on the Life Ledger process.

I asked him, "Where have you been the most disciplined in your life? Not in the gang, not in jail, where did you feel like you did your best?"

He said, "Football practice. When I went to practice, I was successful."

"Tony," I said, "if you write down your goals and do the activities, you *will* reach your goals."

"Alright, Frosty. I'm in."

And he was. I knew his current struggles had nothing to do with his education, his past, or the fact that he didn't have a fat rolodex at his fingertips. He cleaned better than anyone I knew, and he was smart; he just needed structure, goals, and the ability to follow through. Tony needed to make sense of his life.

I had him sit down and write out everything he did all day, in thirty-minute increments. He saw that he was wasting his time with anything other than cleaning offices. The other odd jobs he was saying yes to paid less and were less predictable, which was causing him more stress and eating away at the time he could spend more productively and more happily in other ways. He started really seeing where his time was going, and it was eye-opening for us both. He stopped taking the side jobs and focused on the office cleaning.

Then we looked at his goals. It took more than an hour and a half of my asking what he wanted, what he wanted to get out of his business, and what he wanted for his life. Finally, he told me, "I want to make $15,000 a month."

"Great!" I said, "What else?"

He paused. "I want to take my family to Disney World twice a year."

"Great! What else?"

He paused again. "I want to pay off my house."

"Awesome. What else?"

"I want to write a book!"

"Great. Let's get started on all that!"

We wrote down all his goals and then made a list of what he had to do every single day to make those goals happen. We worked on making phone calls to get new clients and using existing clients as leads. He made at least a call to a new person every single day.

It worked. He found new clients. He went from earning $2,300 a month from just me to $10,000 a month from multiple clients. Once he saw what was possible, he upped his goal to $20,000 a month. He paid off his mortgages and he took his family on that trip to Disney World. He even had to hire two employees to keep up with the demand for his office-cleaning business.

And that book wasn't a throwaway goal. Once he told me that he wanted to be an author, I asked him to make one of his daily activities writing down something to put in the book—a story from his past, thoughts on an experience, lessons he learned. When he is ready to make the book happen, the hard work will already be done.

If you just write down your goals twice a day, if you execute the Ledger, you—just like Tony—will reach your goals. If you're doing those things on a daily basis, the Life Ledger is going to end up changing your life, because it will change the way you think and change the way you're going about your daily business. It will, in short, create intentionality for every single day of your life, which is the secret to opportunity, success, and happiness.

In this book, I'm going to teach you exactly how to write your goals. I'm also going to teach you how to match up those goals with behaviors and activities. I'm going to teach you what activities you're doing during the day that are a liability to you and your goals, and what activities are assets to you reaching your goals and accomplishing your daily tasks.

Everybody talks about going to the next level, but what are the trigger points for that next level? You're going to learn exactly what those are, and what the next level looks and feels like. You're going to learn how to identify problems that are holding you back. You're going to learn exactly what steps you need to take to fix those problems.

The Daily Ledger is going to establish discipline in your life like you've never had before. After reading this book, you'll change your daily routine. You'll start to write down your goals and your targets. You'll start writing down what you're grateful for. You're going to create intentionality in your daily routine that will change your life. All of this will help you to be more accountable in relationships and in your business. And in order to grow and scale your business, you have to have those two things. And by the end of this book, once you've applied all of what you've learned, you'll arrive at a place where you're going to be able to live your ideal life.

John Maxwell, one of my favorite teachers, once said, "When you change your daily routine, you change your life." Are you ready? You're about to change yours.

CHAPTER 2

The Importance of Goal Setting

MY GRANDFATHER WAS A CPA. My father is a CPA. And I am becoming one of the most sought-after CPAs in my profession. Accounting is the fundamental language of business, and I am a natural speaker. Each tax return reveals to me the business owner's best-kept secrets. Each one tells a story of success, failure, or—worse—complacency. In each set of a firm's books, I can tell if owners are setting daily tasks, if they hold themselves accountable, and whether they know how to pair actions with the most important ingredient for success: goals.

A company without goals is just treading water—operating to survive, not to thrive. Eventually, a company without goals will start to tread more slowly and, ultimately, sink. The same can be said for people. We all need goals to keep us moving forward, to keep us energized, happy, and thriving because goals give us something to work toward, to live for. Goals give our life purpose.

What's crazy, though, is that as vital as goals are to our happiness, so many of us don't have them—at least not in the way that leads to real change and accomplishment. Too often the goals we set for ourselves are vague and abstract. "I want to be a millionaire." "I want to travel the world." "I want to find true love." Many people might consider these "goals," but they're not. They're throwaway lines for people who haven't really thought about what they want—or how they will get there. Who doesn't want to have a million dollars? Who wouldn't travel the world if they could? Who doesn't want to find true love?

The problem isn't setting huge goals. You should. I want you to think big. I like setting goals that make my stomach churn a little bit. Huge goals keep motivating you toward growth. But huge goals also require daily action. My sobriety teaches me every day that not drinking for the rest of my life means not drinking today.

So huge goals? Yes, but you have to make them specific to you, and in order to do that, you have to know *why* you want to achieve this goal and *how* you're going to go about doing it.

This is where the Life Ledger comes in.

As an accountant, my entire life has been built around accountability, to-do lists, and the creation of daily activities to reach whatever goals I have at the time. I was taught from a young age that you need at least five things that you must do each day to get what you want in life. My oldest memory is of my father carrying around a yellow note pad, his to-do list clearly written, neat and fresh each day. He started and ended his days with his to-do list, checking items off as he got things done. When I was in elementary school, I would go to my dad's office and sneak into the supply closet to get my own yellow note pad. I learned how to write things down in a way that forced me to accomplish things. "Getting an 'A' on an English paper" was a goal—in fact, since I wasn't the greatest student, especially in English class, this was a pretty darn big goal for me. But wanting something isn't nearly enough. I had to figure how I was going to achieve it.

Like a lot of kids, schoolwork wasn't something I was dying to do every day. So if I was going to get an "A" on an essay, I needed a plan; that "A" wasn't just going to fall out of the sky in a ring of gold stars. So rather than put off reading the books assigned in class until the very last minute, I started a to-do list that said I had to read at least ten pages a day, every day, even on the weekends. And on top of that, after every chapter I had to summarize what I thought it was about and what seemed most important to me. I did this all year long, and my grades on my essays started to improve. It didn't happen overnight, but I did eventually get my "A." And it was one of the best memories I ever had in school. Why? Because I set a big goal, created a plan, and followed it through to the end. There's no better feeling than that. Ultimately, I learned early in life that you must determine your daily actions in order to actually accomplish something. This is exactly what the Life Ledger does.

It starts, first, with some deep self-reflection. Oftentimes, what we say we want, we don't really want. We come up with the easy go-to for what many people generally want: more money, fame, a life of leisure. But in order to create a set of goals for yourself that will actually make you happier and feel more fulfilled, you have to go beyond the easy responses and think more deeply about what *you* truly value in life, what *you* truly want.

This is something I worked on with a client of mine, Katie. We started where I start with all my clients—asking the very basic question: "What do you want?"

Almost immediately, she said, "I want to build a one-hundred-million-dollar company."

"Okay, that's great," I said. "So, why?"

She looked at me for a second, kind of like it was a stupid question. "Because I want to make a lot of money."

"Sure, I totally get that.... But why?"

"Because I want to be able to provide for my family," she said, thinking a bit more deeply.

And it's at this point that you really have to push yourself. The moment you start scratching the surface of *why* you want to do something is when you have to go all-in on thinking it through—because that's where the heart of what really matters to you is. So I didn't let Katie off the hook. I wanted to push her to think even more deeply about her *why*. "Being able to provide for your family is immensely important, of course," I said. "But why do you need to build a one-hundred-million-dollar company to do that?"

She paused now. I could see her really starting to think it all through. "Well, because I want to be able to do what I want to do, when I want to do it."

"And what is it that you actually want to do with this freedom? What is it that you'll do that will make you most happy?"

I could see that a lightbulb went on for Katie in this moment. Her eyes welled up with emotion. "I want to spend more time with my son," she said.

I gave her a moment, and then said, "I hope these are tears of joy, because you are now so much closer to achieving what you value most in your life: spending time with your son."

And that's how her Life Ledger began—not with writing down "I want a one-hundred-million-dollar company," but rather "I want to spend more time with my son." She wrote it down every day, twice a day, and guess what happened? She did. She started arranging her days in ways that would allow her to prioritize quality time with her son. Sometimes that meant going into the office early so she could leave when her son got out of school; sometimes that meant simply putting down whatever project she was working on so she could go to the game or the play or whatever event she might've skipped in the past to do work instead; sometimes it meant taking a personal day or an extended weekend. Basically, the Life Ledger quickly helped Katie realize that if she was ever going to achieve her goal of spending time with her son, she had to make that goal happen right then, on a daily basis. As John Maxwell said, by changing her daily routine, Katie was able to change her life.

To help you probe what your goals truly are, you should break them down into three different categories: personal, professional, and financial. Think through what you want in each and write them down.

For personal, think through what you truly value in your life. What brings you the most joy? The most personal satisfaction? Sometimes it helps to discover what you value most by thinking of what life would be like without something. As the old saying goes, you don't know how good you had it until it's gone. So if you're having trouble thinking of what you want in your personal life, try subtracting things that you already have and consider how you'd feel. If it seems like it wouldn't matter that much if it were gone, then you know it's something you don't place a high value on. If it seems impossible, inconceivable, to not have that thing in your life, then you know you value it greatly and perhaps should consider how you can enhance that value through goal setting.

And don't think it has to be some world-changing goal either. Sometimes we create mental and creative barriers by trying to think of the "coolest" goal or most magnificent goal. It's fine to set big, huge goals, but it's fine to set modest goals too—especially in our personal lives. Maybe you'll discover you want a new home, or you want a family, or you want to take a trip to Israel. Those are all pretty big goals. Or maybe you'll discover that you want to have Saturdays all to yourself or read one new book a month or start learning how to cook. Those are smaller, but still very important in helping to shape the life you want for yourself. Big or small, if it's something you value and will bring you satisfaction and joy in your personal life, write it down.

For professional goals, consider whatever industry you're in, or an industry you want to be in. If you own a business already, consider what you want to accomplish in your business. What are you trying to create? What product have you not created yet that you want to create? How many employees or team members do you want to have at your business? What size do you want your real estate portfolio? Do you want it to be ten units, 10,000 units, 20,000 units?

If you don't own a company, consider what you want out of your current job. Do you want to take on a new role? Do you want a promotion? Do you want to develop new job skills? Or do you want to change jobs altogether? Start a new career? Move to a new company?

For financial goals, ask yourself what you truly want out of your personal economy. Do you want to save enough to retire by the age of fifty-five? Great, write that down. Do you want to be earning six figures a year? Write that down. Are you hoping to pay for your kids' college tuition? Saving up enough for a luxurious cruise? Invest more? Write it down.

The great part about breaking down your goals into these three categories is that you'll often start to find connections between them. You might see that what's really important to you in your personal life is something you might be able to also execute in the goals you set for your professional life. For example, you might find that you want to spend more of your personal time helping the poor or the homeless in your community, and that you also set a goal for your business to be more engaged philanthropically. Having written down these goals for these two categories, it might become plainly obvious to you that you can serve your community even better by shifting your business philanthropy to align with your personal philanthropy. But that's only obvious after you've taken the time to write them down so the goals become more tangible and real.

Or you might find that, like Katie, you want to spend more time with your family as a personal goal, and that you also want to shift your business model to allow more flexibility for your employees during the week. You might find that you can align the two by creating a "Family and Friends" Friday once a month, where everybody has a half-day. In this way, you're starting to not only achieve your goals but also bring more harmony to the different facets of your life, which might help further clarify what you want in your life, or your next set of goals.

Finally, what's important in all three categories is to set *specific* goals. The more focused you can be in listing your goals for each category, the better and the more accurate your goals will be. You need to be able to literally see your goals and how they will manifest in your own life. "Spending more time with family" is an abstraction, for example. It's something many of us say. But because *everyone* says it, it's not personalized to you. However, as in Katie's case, the lightbulb went on when she said she wanted to spend more time with her *son*. At that time in her life, it was her relationship with her son that was most important—and she was able to immediately start executing on that goal. When she wrote it down every day, she knew exactly who she wanted to spend time with and arranged her daily life to make that happen.

But here's the thing: goals aren't just one thing. Goals—especially big, bold goals—are made up of many different things, and they aren't accomplished in hours or days, but each hour and day counts toward getting close to your goal. You should consider every second of your time one step closer to achieving your goal. But to do that, you need daily, actionable items that will help you get there.

A friend of mine, Kyle, wanted to be a better father. That was his goal. We were speaking casually at the time, and I told him that writing down that goal every day would help. And he did. He wrote "I want to be a better father" every day in his to-do list—but didn't do anything more than that. A few weeks later we met up for lunch and he said, "I write my goal down every day, twice a day. I'm as busy as ever, but I don't feel like I am accomplishing anything."

The problem for Kyle is that he didn't have any actionable items to get him closer to his goal. He set a lofty goal with no means of getting there. Part of goal setting is also thinking through the smaller, incremental, daily steps you can take to achieve your goal. I call them Daily Targets, or DTs.

So we evaluated this goal together. I tried to help him figure out what being a "better father" meant to him, and how that would look to him each day. That was when the lightbulb went on for him. He could start to see his path. The first DT he wrote down was "Tucking my kids into bed every night." He was a workaholic, and so his second DT was "Making sure I'm home for dinner each night." Kyle was Christian, and he felt part of being a good father would also be to be a better Christian. His third DT was to "Read a section of the Bible every day." Once he got rolling, there was no stopping him.

After that, he wasn't just writing down his goals, he actually did the work. A few weeks later, Kyle came to me. "This is completely changing my life. If there is ever a change in course in my life, I need to change the action, not just say I want to reach my goals." His confidence as a father has never been more strong or secure.

I recently had a client named Beth, whose first goal was "Travel to five new places."

"That's great," I said, "but how do you get to these places?" She looked at me puzzled at first. "I mean, are you going to take a bus? A plane? Train?"

"Well, I don't know," she said. "I don't know what places I'm going to yet."

"Exactly!" I said. "You need to. If you can't see the place in your mind, if you don't know exactly where you want to go, you'll never get there." It didn't take long for Beth to figure out the places she wanted to go, and she began writing them down, twice a day. But she also created a list of DTs to help her work toward that goal each day. Every day, she committed to doing research on at least one of her destinations. She was checking out airfares, hotels, and best times of year to visit for each place. Within six months, she had already taken her first trip.

Mikaela also had another goal to make more income. I asked her to list exactly how much more income she wanted annually. After we did that, we started working on a list of DTs that would help her achieve this goal. Beth was in sales, so networking and putting herself out there were instrumental to her business success. So, she wrote down a DT: "Developing a bigger professional network." But Mikaela was quieter and a little more introverted, so networking was way outside of her comfort zone. This was so out of her comfort zone that I made her write down additional, more concrete DTs. She did. She joined multiple networking organizations in her field, she began going to sales seminars, and she committed to reaching out to at least one person a day. It didn't take long before she started getting more referrals, which lead to more commissions, which lead to more income.

The Life Ledger for Mikaela's goal became the action that made these goals her reality. And as I said, writing down your goals every day helps you to see things that weren't apparent before. Writing down her goals every day in the Life Ledger allowed her to see the connections between the different categories of her goals. For example, as Mikaela began traveling more, she increased her knowledge of different places and developed a library of new stories and experiences— not only about the places themselves, but the stories of booking hotels or hassles at the airport or meeting cool new people. And guess what? Having all these stories and experiences helped her professional networking. She was able to relate to people on new and different levels, sharing funny stories about scenic roads in Mexico or travel nightmares at Heathrow Airport. Ultimately, her income grew *because* of her personal goal of traveling more.

So now that you're starting to understand the importance of goal setting, as well as how vital writing down these goals is every day, the next big part is the conviction to see it all through. Building conviction is critical to achieving the goals you set for yourself, which is why we're going to talk about that now.

CHAPTER 3

Building Conviction

IT'S ONE THING TO SET a goal, but if you don't love it, or your heart's just not into it, let's be real: your chances of accomplishing it are essentially zero. Chances are you'll probably go back to doing what you did before, if you changed anything at all to begin with. And if you've gotten caught up in the day-to-day operations of your life, you probably are pretty disconnected from the passion that drove you to set goals for yourself in the first place. This chapter is about helping you to remember your true passion and the way to spark it into action.

To do this, you need to build conviction. But like achieving goals, building conviction doesn't happen all at once. It's not like in the movies when suddenly, at the start of the final act, awesome inspirational music starts playing and the hero saves the world and finds true love in the next thirty minutes. Conviction is something you need to work on and cultivate over time.

Building conviction is a lot like building a fire. You have to start small, with tiny twigs and kindling, so that a spark has a chance to ignite a small flame. Then you must have the patience to let that small flame grow. You have to monitor it, protect it, blow on it to keep it going. Then as it catches on, you can slowly start building, adding on bigger sticks, growing the flame higher and hotter. Then and only then, after you've put in the time, will you be rewarded with a burning fire that will last all night long. And once it does, it's so much easier to reignite it the next day because all the embers are still hot, still burning. That foundation is in place for you to move on and do other things.

It's the same thing with conviction. You need to start smaller, with Daily Targets (DTs), to allow that spark to take hold. Then you have to have the patience to see that small flame through. You might want everything to happen all at once—we all do. And when it doesn't happen as fast as we would like, we can get discouraged or disappointed or angry, and then our conviction, like that small starter flame for the fire, starts to waver and wane. It can go out as quickly as it appeared. But if you stick with it, if you're persistent and patient, and commit to the smaller targets that will ultimately lead you to your bigger goals, you will succeed, because you will have built the conviction to see it through to the end. And, like that first fire, once the foundation is there, you can achieve anything.

So, let's get that fire started!

First, as with most things, to truly figure out where you're going, you have to figure out where you've been. How, exactly, are you spending your days? I have all of my clients start out with this exercise. I call it Life Mapping, and I talk about this process in detail in Chapter 5. But let me provide you with a brief over-view for now. Map out a timeline of an entire week of your life at thirty-minute intervals—the full twen-ty-four hours. So start at, say, 6 a.m. and write down what you did every thirty minutes thereafter every day for seven straight days. It's better to start at a set point and go the full twenty-four hours so that you can also see if you're sleeping too much or too little. And don't cheat. At every thirty-minute interval, write down what you're doing. Every minute of your day should count for something. Every thirty minutes. Every day. Full week. No cheating.

This should give you a full enough picture for you to start evaluating how you spend your time—and, more importantly, if these are activities that are helping you to achieve what you want in life, if these are activities that can help you achieve your goals.

As an accountant, I'm trained to look at the activities of my clients in two ways: assets or liabilities. The definition of an asset is that it provides future benefit to you. The definition of liability is it's a future detriment to you. In this case, as you evaluate the map of your daily life, you need to think of each activity in these terms: either it's an asset that is helping you achieve your goals and the life you want for yourself, or it's a liability that is preventing you from achieving your goals and the life you want for yourself.

Create two columns: one for assets, the other for liabilities. Then go through your daily life map and put each activity into one of these two columns. I call this process Life Auditing, and I talk more about this in detail in Chapter 6.

So how do you identify something as an asset versus a liability? It depends on your goals, and it depends on you as a person. Everyone is different. Ultimately, your daily activities should align with your goals. So, for example, you might find out that you spend four thirty-minute increments, two hours of your day, binging *Game of Thrones*. If your goal is to be an aspiring actor or a fantasy fiction writer, you might well place this activity in the asset column because you're learning about your craft by watching one of the most famous shows of all time. On the other hand, for many people binging shows like this might be more of a distraction than anything else, in which case you'd put it in the liability column; it's not helping *you* to reach *your* particular goals.

But life's complicated, we're all complicated. We have different wants and needs. We have different ways of doing things, of being productive. Some people are morning people; they open their eyes and are immediately ready to conquer the world. Other people need two showers and five cups of coffee before they can utter a word. But those same people might be fully energized at 9 p.m., while the morning people can barely keep their eyes open. We're different. We operate differently. And that's okay. The trick is to identify what *you* need to optimize *your* productivity.

This was something I had to (and continue to) work through myself. Like, for me, I actually need a little distraction in my day. I wish I could stay focused 24/7 on whatever it is I need to be doing, but I can't. I found that if I try to do that, I actually end up becoming *less* productive—and once that happens, I'm actually wasting time and energy that would be better spent elsewhere. So I've spent my life examining and trying to work through my liabilities.

Drinking was of course a big one. A beast actually. And it took me years to accept I had a problem, but now that I have, now that I have admitted I need help and the support of friends, family, and colleagues, I've been able to replace that tremendous liability with so many more constructive DTs.

Social media is another. And it's a tricky one because I need social media to build and scale my businesses. In some ways, it's an asset. But then there are the many times I'm not really being constructive with my use of social media. I get distracted and start clicking on random YouTube videos or checking out my friends' Instagram accounts. Before I know it, an hour's gone by and I haven't done a thing. My asset has now become a liability.

Watching TV is another. I kind of need that time to just chill and do nothing. The problem is when I'd be binging seven straight hours of *Breaking Bad*. Day gone.

But because I know that about myself, because I know I'm prone to distraction—yet need a little distraction to optimize my daily productivity—I schedule distraction into my day. But I make sure that I don't overdo it! An hour of *Game of Thrones* (two thirty-minute segments) is okay; ten thirty-minute segments is not.

Knowing these things about yourself—your vices and distractions as well as your strengths—will help you immensely in this process. The main thing is to be honest with yourself. If you lie to yourself, the only person you're hurting is you. Keep all of this in mind as you examine your activities in terms of assets and liabilities. Consider your goals, consider your values, and consider your personality. If you don't keep it real, if you're not true to yourself, it won't work.

Once you've completely broken down your daily life map into assets and liabilities, it's time to start zeroing in on getting rid of the liabilities. Many people find that their day is being filled with more liabilities than assets, with things that are preventing them from achieving what they want rather than things that are helping them. The more liabilities you can get rid of in your daily routine, the more time you have to spend on constructive daily targets that will help you achieve your goals.

What you'll also find is that assets help build conviction. Assets make you feel good about yourself. Assets invigorate you, energize you, help you grow stronger— all of the things that will help you reach and achieve your goals. Liabilities, on the other hand, do the opposite. Liabilities make us feel worse about ourselves, make us doubt ourselves. Liabilities impede our progress each day, and so they impede our progress in life.

In order to get my life back after I had hit rock bottom, I did this same exact asset-liability evaluation. I was astounded to see how much of my time was spent on liabilities. At my lowest point, almost all of my time was spent on things that were ultimately not making me happy—in fact, I was spending almost all of my time on things that were making me increasingly unhappy.

I was drinking too much, and then as a result, I was sleeping too much. To compensate for those liabilities, I was almost exclusively dedicating all of my time at work in operating mode. I tried to micromanage everything, every day, all the time, out of a fear that my failings in my personal life would bleed into my professional life. Both suffered as a result.

Once I started replacing the liabilities with productive DTs, I was able to slowly regain my footing in my life. It didn't happen in a day, or a week, or a month. But each day gave me a little more strength and hope to face the next day. And that day gave me the strength to face the day after that. And slowly my conviction, like that small flame in the kindling, began to build and grow stronger. The stronger my conviction became, the more I was able to do each day. And the more I was able to do each day, the closer I got to achieving my goals.

Recently, I went through these steps all over again to break out the asset expenses and liability expenses in all of my businesses. I even had to determine who was a liability to the company and who was an asset. My management team and I created the new list of assets only and started implementing the steps. We focused only on asset actions and quit the liability actions completely. We rerouted the ship for our accounting firm, and now we have a plan to execute. It was amazing to see the progress we have made in such a short period of time. Once I saw those two lists side by side—all of the assets versus all of the liabilities—everything just clicked.

Most people have zero plans to reach their goals; they are just trying to stay afloat. While the assets buoy them up, their liabilities are dragging them down. They can never actually swim anywhere. I untied my liabilities and let them sink away. It was freeing and transformational.

So before we get into the step-by-step process of how this all works, let's review what we've learned so far.

🜍 Every change in your life—for worse or for better—begins with you. The Life Ledger is the tool you need to enact positive change in your life. It will set you on a daily path that will enable you to prioritize, focus, and invest your time wisely so that you're moving the needle each and every day.

🜍 Setting big, bold goals is the first step. Writing these goals down every day, twice a day, will keep you laser-focused on what's important in your life and what you want out of it.

🜍 But it's not enough to merely write down the goals, you also need actionable steps to help you get there. We call those Daily Targets, or DTs. These are the smaller, incremental, daily actions you can take that will get you closer to your goal.

🜨 Once you've established your goals and your DTs, it's time to figure out where you've been in order to figure out where you're going. Start by Life Mapping out a week of your life. List every activity you took part in within thirty-minute increments for the duration of your Life Mapping period.

🜨 Once you have this week fully broken down, it's time to start evaluating these activities in terms of assets and liabilities by doing your Life Audit. Ultimately, you'll assign all of your daily activities to either the asset column or the liability column.

🜨 By the end of this process, you want to replace all of your liabilities with DTs that will help you be more productive, which in turn builds strength and the conviction to keep working, to keep striving for your best life, your best self. This is what I call an asset-only life, and I'll talk more about this in Chapter 7.

🜨 Once you begin to transform your life and achieve your goals, I'll show you how to take your success with the Life Ledger to the next

level. This is a step that induces a lot of anxiety in people, but I'll explain why it's not
actually scary at all and why it is absolutely
essential to achieving all that you want in life.

⚡ Your daily plan will then be to write—twice
a day, every day—in the Life Ledger your
goals and the DTs that will get you there.
This daily practice will keep your plan top of
mind and continue sustaining your conviction and passion to accomplish all that you
want in life.

⚡ The final two chapters of the book I dedicate
to providing you with concrete strategies to
not only grow your wealth but also protect it
over time. It's important to understand that
just because you might generate a lot of revenue it doesn't mean you're also creating a
lot of wealth. The two don't necessarily go
hand in hand, as we hear all the time about
famous people, rich people, who end up with
nothing. I'll provide you with simple, effective strategies you can follow to make your
money work for you while also providing
you with the knowledge to protect what you
earn over the span of your life.

Before we go into detail about each step of the Life Ledger process, I want to reveal to you an often-over-looked aspect of finding true happiness and unimaginable success in life. I call it the X Factor.

THE X FACTOR

So you're understanding the importance of setting goals and you're building conviction to not only set these ambitious goals for yourself but also the will to see them through. There's one very important final component I need to share with you before we explore in detail the steps of the Life Ledger process. I call it the X Factor.

I discovered the X Factor at a low point in my life, and at the time, it was a lifeline—what I literally needed to pull myself out of the hole I had dug for myself in life, what I needed to survive. But over time I've discovered it's much more than that. It's gone from being a lifeline I've needed to survive to the key, critical element that is essential in order to thrive.

So what is this mystical factor that can be all things at once? It's a couple of things actually.

The first part of the X Factor is humility. More specifically, it's the understanding that you can't control everything in your life—which of course requires humility. The day I realized this was the day I stopped drinking for good. As I told you, I was trying really hard to quit drinking, or at least cut down on my drinking. I would play all sorts of mind games with myself—to only drink this, or only drink that, or only drink during these days, or this time of day, or whatever. But it was never really the right actions that were required in order to overcome my problem. The thing is, for the longest time, my operating was keeping me afloat. Despite all my internal struggles, despite my drinking habit that was slowly dragging me down, I was actually fairly successful. I had a beautiful, loving wife, I had two amazing children, I was a successful CPA. On the surface, as I said, things were looking pretty good. And because they were looking pretty good, I was fooling myself into thinking they actually were pretty good. Basically, I was full of myself. I believed I was in control, that I was the master of my own destiny, that I had life right where I wanted it. Yes, I definitely had moments where I felt the exact opposite, and I think deep down I knew I was off track, but delusion is a powerful thing, and admitting weakness can be extremely difficult—at least it was for me.

But there was that moment where it all came crashing down on me—the reality that things weren't going great, that I wasn't truly happy, that my drinking was in fact a problem—a big problem that was only getting bigger, consuming more of me, more of my life, more of my happiness. I had to accept the fact that I in fact didn't have control—of any of it. I had to admit to myself, *I can't control this.*

So, in business and in life, there are a lot of times where we come across these different challenges. They may not be as extreme as my experience, but we face challenges all the time. Life happens. There are so many things that come across our desk or come across our counter at home, and we just don't have any control over it. There are so many experiences in life that we just can't control, and it's incredibly important to admit that to yourself, to have the humility to understand that you can't control everything all the time.

And I have a chapter about this because I know in many parts of the Life Ledger process I'm explaining to you how your life is in your control—and it is!— but that doesn't disqualify the realities in life and the respect you need to have for your place in it. Having humility is foundational to this understanding. When people lack humility, they end up with a false sense of self, and that can have far-reaching consequences not only for being happy with yourself—that is, being truly happy with who you are as a person—but it can also present obstacles to achieving all that you want in life, oftentimes in ways you might not ever know. For example, people who lack humility think they control everything, that nobody is as good or as smart or as powerful as them. That kind of aura is repellent. One way or another, a person who lacks humility will create distance and detachment from those around them. Sometimes it might be that person literally keeping people at arm's length. Other times those other people will simply stay away from that person who lacks humility. In either case, this person is missing out on creating potentially valuable relationships that could advance them further in life.

Let me give you an example of how this works. One of my clients, Lucas, came to me, and I could tell right away that he lacked humility, that he thought he was better than everyone else. Even though he came to me for help, he was acting as if it were the other way around. He was bragging about his accomplishments, all the people he "beat" in life, all the challenges he "beat" in life. Basically, the first hour we were together was him telling me over and over how great he was.

Finally, I flatly asked him, "So why are you here?"

Lucas looked at me kind of confused. "What do you mean?"

I repeated the question. "Why are you here?"

He got this annoyed look on his face, like I was trying to make him say something that he didn't want to say. "You know why I'm here. Why else would I be here?"

"People come to see me for lots of reasons," I said. "In my experience, I've learned that asking questions is the best way to begin understanding people. Which is why I'm asking you this simple question now: Why are you here?"

It took him a while. I could tell he was really struggling with having to say it, but that was exactly the point. He desperately needed to say it. He needed to come to this realization, and to do it, he needed to say it out loud and to someone else. (This is something I talk about later in the book: the need to speak to and trust other people in overcoming your liabilities.) "I need help," he said.

And that was it. From that moment on, all the bravado began to disappear. All the walls that Lucas had put up throughout his life started to come down. I very quickly got to know his true self. And to be clear, Lucas is extremely talented. He is a very bright guy. But he also has his weaknesses, his liabilities. Like everyone else in the world, he has his flaws and his problems. He needs other people just like we all do, and he needs to know that about himself. He needs humility.

After about six months of doing the Life Ledger, Lucas seemed like an entirely different person. We met for lunch one day, and he came in super excited.

He sits down and looks as giddy as a little kid. "You're not going to believe this," he said.

Lucas had spent so much time in his life trying to push people away that he ended up feeling isolated and alone in his life. What started out as a defense mechanism when he was younger ended up consuming who he became as an adult. So one of his first goals in his Life Ledger might seem basic to you, but was a very big deal to him. It read: Make meaningful connections with others.

When he started writing that down in his Life Ledger every day, he began in the weeks and months that followed to make a concerted effort to do just that. He started taking time to actually talk to and learn about his employees (he owned a company). And through those conversations, he began to see them not merely as "employees," but as real people, with real lives, with real concerns, and also with real good ideas for helping the business—things that he never would have thought of himself. But this one particular instance that he was telling me about at lunch had to do with one of his middle managers, Brandon, who he actually started to become friends with outside of work.

"So Brandon calls me up a couple of weeks ago and says he scored two awesome seats for the game and asks if I want to go with him." Lucas then pauses and looks at me. "Now, JD, what would I normally have done before I started the Life Ledger?"

I laughed. "There's no way in hell you would've gone."

"Exactly!" he says. "No way I go. It's a Thursday night. I gotta work the next day. Hockey's not even really my thing. But I thought about my goals. I thought about my need to make real connections with people, and so I said yes."

"Good for you!" I said.

"Yeah, I mean, that was a small thing. But I've been making those decisions consistently all the time, and I'm one hundred percent happier for it. Brandon and I really did have a great time. He's a great guy, and I'm thankful I can call him a friend now. But here's the thing: we're at the game, and the seats he got are right next to these two guys in the box next to us. The four of us got to talking, and it turns out they're investment bankers who were loving what our company does. They love what we're about." He pauses, beaming. "They called me yesterday and we set up a meeting for next week to explore some opportunities they see for us. I mean, if this isn't proof the Life Ledger works, I don't know what is!"

This is obviously a huge success story (the bankers invested heavily in Lucas's firm), but it would absolutely never have happened if Lucas hadn't taken that first very basic step of acknowledging he can't control everything, of showing humility. It's what kicked off his entire Life Ledger journey.

Humility is the first part of the X Factor because it's a game changer in how you perceive life and everyone around you. Once you realize you can't control everything, that you do in fact need other people, you don't have to prove anything to anybody anymore. You can just be who you are. Play to your strengths and mitigate your weaknesses, without having to hide from them. I no longer have to prove how much control I have or how "together" I am or pretend that I have all the answers. That takes up so much time and energy and cognitive space—all of which would be far better spent trying to innovate and create.

But don't get me wrong. It's not easy to do. It does take time to accept that you don't have all the answers, that you don't have all the control. It's difficult, and sometimes frightening, to say there's no way I'm going to be able to control every situation and every aspect of life. It starts with small things. Daily things. Set your mind to controlling what you set your mind to control. Saying, "Okay, I did it today. I did that one thing today." The sooner that you can accept that you're not going to be able to do everything in one day, that you can't control everything all the time, the sooner you can start organizing your day to day and control only those things.

This is what the Daily Ledger is, it is clarifying for you what you do have control over every day no matter what happens, and those items are aligned with your goals, which will then allow you to reach your goals.

And it begins with that acknowledgement of humility as the first part of the X Factor.

And this humility leads to the second part of the X Factor: a growth mindset.

There's been a lot of research on the importance of having a growth mindset in all aspects of life. But to understand what a growth mindset is, you have to understand its exact counterpoint: a fixed mindset. A fixed mindset is believing, first and foremost, that intelligence is a fixed trait. That might not sound like a huge deal, but it actually leads to a whole slew of other things that undercut a person's ability to reach their full potential and achieve all that they want in life.

For example, people who have a fixed mindset and believe intelligence is a fixed trait are likely to also believe that they are naturally good at something or naturally bad at something. This kind of mentality leads to avoidance and crushes motivation—the exact opposite of what is required for innovation and entrepreneurship. To show my clients how this works, I use simple, everyday examples that anyone can relate to. Take dancing. Let's say Emma, who has a fixed mindset in life, believes she's a really bad dancer. She believes she has no rhythm, has no ear for music, is uncoordinated, etc. Because she believes she's naturally not gifted in this respect, she never tries to get better. In fact, she avoids dancing altogether. This avoidance, however, isn't restricted only to the act of dancing; it also bleeds into all the other facets of life that dancing might be a part of. At parties, Emma stays clear of the dance floor, even when all of her friends are having a blast in the middle of it all night long. She gets stressed and anxious about formal events because she's afraid she will be required to dance or that someone might ask her to dance. Even though she is a very kind, polite person with a good sense of humor, she sometimes appears rude to other people because of how much she tries to avoid revealing what she considers to be her lack of dancing ability. Basically, her fixed mindset when it comes to this one simple thing actually has profound consequences in many aspects of her emotional and social life, which could end up having consequences in even more aspects of her life.

But this is just one small implication of having a fixed mindset. There are a lot more problems that could arise. People with fixed mindsets also tend to give up easily when faced with a setback. They tend to get more jealous of other people's successes because they view them as superior natural attributes in others and thus feel worse about themselves (for not having the same natural attributes). Consequently, they also tend to take constructive feedback poorly because they view it as a personal criticism rather than a suggestion for a way to improve. Ultimately, people with fixed mindsets see things in a zero-sum type of way. It's all or nothing. They either dance well or they don't. They're good at math or they're not. They have a knack for raising kids or they don't. They're exceptional at starting new businesses or they're awful. There are no degrees in a fixed mindset, which all comes down to the false belief of needing to control everything.

When you're trying to learn something new, you have to accept that you're going to fail in the process. There's simply no other way to get better at something. We learn through failure. That's just the way it works. But if you believe that you can't get better at something, then there's really no sense in trying, right? It's hopeless. To compensate, a person with a fixed mindset tries to control as much as they can all the time. It's restrictive, however, because to never learn new things means you have to withdraw from the world to some degree—perhaps to a large degree. And that's when you start putting up walls to keep people away so that they can't see your flaws, so that they can't detect your natural weaknesses. It's in large part what had happened to Lucas over time.

Sounds terrible, right? Who would ever want to go through life with that kind of perspective?

Unfortunately, a cold hard truth is that most people have this kind of mindset. Most people have this fixed mentality about who they are and what they can and cannot do in life. It's very likely that you yourself have a fixed mindset. If you've ever said, "I suck at X," or "I'm no good at Y," you're revealing a fixed mindset. Statements like that likely lead you to avoid learning opportunities or trying new things. A fixed mindset is also exactly the type of mentality that leads to operating. We "stay in our lane" and do what we know we're good at, never branching out, shutting off opportunities for growth and collaboration in spaces that feel less comfortable to us.

A growth mindset, on the other hand, is required to build, innovate, create, and thrive. In contrast to a fixed mindset, a growth mindset is one that considers intelligence a facet of oneself that can be enhanced and improved with hard work and determination. A person with a growth mindset embraces flaws and weaknesses and commits to making them strengths, or, at the very least, improving upon them.

To show how a growth mindset works in comparison to a fixed mindset, let's revisit the story of Emma from earlier. Let's say that Emma has a growth mindset rather than a fixed mindset. Rather than viewing her lack of talent for dance as something fixed and unchangeable about herself, Emma can acknowledge her challenges but also embrace the possibility of improving as a dancer. To do so, she leans into the experience rather than running away from it. She takes dance classes twice a week. She openly accepts tips and suggestions from her friends. She's able to laugh at herself at parties, which people find endearing. She also meets so many more people by not needing to cordon herself off from others at social gatherings. She's also not constantly anxious and stressed before going to social events or people asking her to dance when she's at them. She's happier as a result. And guess what? She's actually a pretty decent dancer now!

The same cascade of negative consequences that we see with having a fixed mindset also applies to having a growth mindset—except the consequences are all positive. People who have a growth mindset and believe they can improve themselves in all areas of life through hard work are also far more motivated to try new things and take on new challenges—due to the very fact that they believe they can improve rather than that are destined to fail. And because they believe they can get smarter and overcome weaknesses, they're also far more apt to put in the effort to make that happen. Think about it—if you don't think you can change something about yourself, why would you bother trying? But if you do believe you can change something about yourself, of course you'll put in the time and effort to do just that. People with a growth mindset aren't threatened by other people's achievements (like people with fixed mindsets) because they believe they can work hard to achieve great things as well. In fact, people with growth mindsets are often inspired by people's accomplishments. Finally, people with growth mindsets are also far better at accepting (and implementing) constructive criticism and feedback from others. They invite differing opinions with the understanding that they in fact do not know everything, and that although they have the power to change themselves and improve themselves, there are other people who may still be better at certain things and more knowledgeable about certain things.

And so it's here that we come full circle. To accept these things about yourself in order to improve and get better with the help of others is contingent on the first part of the X Factor: humility. You can't have a growth mindset without humility. It's the foundation from which a growth mindset can flourish. Humility and growth mindset together make up that essential X Factor that will allow you to transform your life and achieve all that you've ever wanted.

Ultimately the X Factor is empowering. But it's empowering in a way that most people don't think of when we think of that word. Far too often, empowering translates to many people as overpowering. To achieve, to win, translates to beating other people through strength and controlling others to get what you want. Perhaps that works for some people, but it will never lead to true happiness and true success. Those achievements have to start from within oneself. You have to know yourself inside and out. You have to know your strengths, of course, but as important—or actually more important—is to know your weaknesses. You need to know what you cannot control, to know where you need help in life, both to better yourself and to reach the goals you set for yourself. That's true strength. That's true character. And that's what so many people do not understand as they try to advance through life. And it's why the X Factor will be such a powerful tool for you as you begin this journey of personal transformation.

Now that you understand the big picture of the Life Ledger and all the qualities it entails, let's take a deeper dive into each specific part of the process.

CHAPTER 4

Step 1: The Creation Foundation

NOW THE QUESTION IS: WHERE to start? And if you're like most people, trying to figure out where to start is often the most difficult part.

But it's important here to think more deeply about the word *start*. Because the idea of *starting* anything can induce fear or anxiety, sometimes so much that we become paralyzed and end up doing nothing at all.

So let's be clear: it's not really the "starting" part that's so difficult. You likely have no trouble starting your car in the morning. You probably don't give a second thought to starting in on whatever project you're currently doing at work. When was the last time you had serious trouble starting to make dinner at night for your family, or starting to scroll through your social media apps before going to sleep? In fact, you're actually really good at starting lots of things. The amount of things you start every day should make you an expert in starting! And once you start these things, they probably run pretty smoothly, as only an expert could do. Once the car is running, you have no problem driving it (hopefully). You do well at your job. Your family seems to be doing just fine in the nourishment department. You're actually amazing at starting things!

The fear doesn't come from the starting part at all; it actually only comes when we have to start something *new*. It's the newness that scares us—and not without reason. Anything new brings some degree of anxiety. When you were a kid, you were sometimes—maybe all the time!—afraid to try new foods. You were nervous before the first day of a new school year or entering a new school altogether. As you get older, newness comes in different forms: maybe a new job, or moving to a new neighborhood, entering into a new relationship, or having to voice your opinion in public for the first time.

So why? Why is new so often so scary to us? It's because we all, to some degree, have a fear of the unknown. It's like as a kid being afraid of the dark. The unknown is that darkness, that void, where we don't quite know where we're going, or how to get there, or how it will turn out. It's like the first time you make a new recipe for dinner. There's always a little more anxiety involved. You check the recipe over and over to make sure you're doing it right because you're not quite sure what the process is, how it should work, and how it's going to turn out. But after you've done it once, the second time is a little easier. You feel a little less nervous. And then after a while, after going through that same process over and over, you're not nervous at all; you probably don't even think about it—you just do it.

If you step back and look at it, the way we learn to do things is quite remarkable. We go from being nervous, uncertain, and self-conscious to confident and self-assured, and we do this all without ever realizing it. We suddenly look back and can't imagine not knowing how to do it in the first place. But that's not a mystical process that occurs—it's science! The repetition of doing something actually creates a roadmap in our brain. That is, the neurons and synapses in our brain rewire over time to create neural pathways to get from point A (say, a bunch of ingredients we never put together before) to point B (all of the ingredients cooked in a way that makes one delicious dish).

And it's this rewiring of the brain, this creation of a roadmap to get to where you want to be, that the Life Ledger does for you. It empowers you to start, maintain, and finish all that you've ever wanted to accomplish in life. But you need to have a daily routine and you need to follow that routine every day. You have to commit to it. And if you do, you'll see how the world lights up right in front of your eyes. And while it may sound somewhat easy to just "write down your goals each day," it's not. It takes discipline and dedication to create and recreate your goals every single day.

So to help get you started, I'm going to provide you with a routine you should follow to build, what I call, a Creation Foundation. These are five simple steps you can do every day to cultivate the focus and dedication you need to achieve the success you want. The five steps are: beating the sun up, morning meditation, exercising, brain training, and writing in the Life Ledger. I call this the Daily Five and committing to it will set you on your way to changing your life.

BEATING THE SUN UP

What do Apple CEO Tim Cook, four-star general Stanley McChrystal, actor Dwayne "The Rock" Johnson, and former First Lady Michelle Obama have in common? Yep, they all beat the sun up.

If "beating the sun up" sounds like the opening salvo to a *Rocky* movie, it's meant to. I want you to attack each day like it's your last, just as all these famous and highly successful people do. If you can start each day by beating the sun up, well, then you're clearly starting each day in the right frame of mind to take no prisoners and accomplish all of your goals.

And I get it, this is going to be easier for some people (morning people) than others (night people), but the vast majority of people—even morning people—don't get up before the sun rises. Very few people beat the sun up. So by doing so, you're already putting yourself into a very select group of people.

And, yes, sleep is important. It replenishes our body and our brain to give us the energy and strength to tackle each day. Most adults should be getting about seven to eight hours of sleep per day. That means you can go to bed at 10 p.m. and sleep most of the year until 6 a.m., get a full eight hours of sleep, and still beat the sun up. Point is, you can do this! And the benefits are immense.

Beating the sun up means you're also beating all your competition up. You're getting started on your day while everyone else is still sleeping. Over time, that becomes a huge advantage. It's like a daily head start, and it's worked wonders for me.

I myself was always a night person. I was happy to stay up late and get up at the last possible moment to go to work and start my day. On the weekends, rolling out of bed just in time for brunch wasn't unusual. But when I think back now about all those wasted hours—hours I stayed up past midnight watching movies and hours I would doze on and off all morning or lie in bed reading my phone—I wince. It's almost painful because I know now how much more productive I've become by regimenting myself to beat the sun up every day.

We all have so many distractions in our days—work obligations, clients calling at odd hours, family events, taxiing the kids back and forth to one thing or another—that it was a revelation when I would wake up at 5:00 a.m. or so, the sky still dark, the house quiet, phone not buzzing, and realize I had this space, this time, all to myself. It was mine. It gave me the time and space to start thinking about what I—me!—wanted, and how I would go about achieving what I wanted.

In short, beating up the sun was a revelation. Most people don't have the discipline to beat the sun up, but so many highly successful people do. A recent poll found that 90 percent of executives and 50 percent of self-made millionaires are up before 6 a.m. Why? Because it works.

I strongly suggest that this is the very first place you start in building your Creation Foundation. It lays the groundwork for everything that follows.

MORNING MEDITATION

This next step goes hand in hand with beating the sun up. The first is to get out of bed. The second—morning meditation—makes sure that you have time built into your day that allows you to think calmly and deeply about your place in this vast, beautiful world we all exist in. It's a time to think about your place in the universe, to be self-reflective and humble.

To be clear, I'm not suggesting some regimented, strict practice. Quite the opposite. Morning meditation can mean lots of different things to different people. It could mean prayer for some, it could mean mindfulness exercises for others, and for others still it could just mean sitting quietly and thinking about whatever comes to mind. You might find that you do all three, or something entirely different. For me as a Christian, I use this time as a devotional. It's helped me become a better Christian and a better person, and it's inspired me to work toward my goals even at my lowest points.

And this doesn't have to take up a lot of your day. My suggestion is to start with a time that's comfortable for you: something that's substantial but not burdensome. Most of my clients seem to fall in the ten-to-thirty-minute range. For those who really enjoy this meditation period, they're more apt to go closer to thirty minutes; for those who find meditative time more challenging, they opt for times closer to ten minutes. I'd suggest ten minutes be your base. That gives you at least enough time to get settled and force yourself to sit and pray or think in solitude every day. And I'd suggest not going much past thirty minutes because you risk abusing that time and not making it as focused and constructive as it should be every day. You don't want this time to become another vice. As you gain more control over your mornings and your meditation, you can then adjust accordingly beyond this range, if you're so inclined.

The important thing is that you set aside some time in your morning just for this quiet solitude. It's an amazing way to center yourself and to maintain a sense of who you are and where you belong. Doing so helps you stay focused not only on what's important in your life, but also what's important in life generally. This is vital to building the discipline and focus to reach your goals.

EXERCISING

With this step, you might be thinking, huh? In order to achieve my goals, I have to run on a treadmill and jump rope every day? Well, yeah, that's pretty much what I'm saying. (The choice of exercise is yours!) Here's the deal: we live in an unnaturally sedentary society. Whereas our ancient ancestors were constantly on the move—

building, hunting, cooking—many of us can sit without moving more than a few feet each day from morning until night. That's not only unhealthy, it's destructive to creativity and ambition.

We have two legs for a reason. We were meant to move about this planet. Our physical well-being depends on it, but, most importantly for our purposes, our mental well-being depends on it too. Most people only think of exercise in terms of building muscle and carving out six-pack abs. But exercise is crucial to mental strength. In essence, building the body also builds the mind.

There are tons of studies that show how physical exercise reduces anxiety and depression while simultaneously improving self-confidence, self-esteem, and mental functioning. It also helps improve our sleep, improve our general mood, and increases our energy level and stamina—all of which are necessary to go that extra mile to achieve all that you want in life.

On top of that, a daily exercise routine also continues to build structure into your day. It creates intention— the intention to continually keep improving yourself, to make yourself stronger and healthier, which in turn will make you happier. Having a structure to your day can't be overstated. We need structure. And we need to fill that structure with activities and behaviors that help us improve ourselves. Physical exercise accomplishes all of this.

As with morning meditation, your daily exercise doesn't have to be an all-day affair. You're not training to be a pro athlete, after all. My suggestion is to set a minimum of thirty minutes of exercise a day and sixty minutes as a maximum. Again, this range can be tweaked once you've fully established a workout routine and you're in control of your process. But thirty minutes will help prevent those who absolutely hate exercising from doing so little that the gains are minimal if anything at all. And a sixty-minute ceiling will prevent people who actually love working out from doing it to excess to avoid doing other activities that they may not be as inclined to do (but are also very important to achieving their goals). So I've found thirty to sixty minutes is a good starter range.

When I started exercising, I was absolutely not a fan. And not being a morning person, the very last thing I wanted to do was wake up and run three miles on a treadmill! But I stuck with it and, as much as I hated it, forced myself to reach the thirty-minute threshold every day. And lo and behold, after a couple of months (it definitely didn't happen overnight!), I actually started to enjoy exercising. I started to like that time just as much as the morning meditation. I felt a certain peace when I was exercising, and I bumped up that time to forty-five minutes. I then tried an hour, but I eventually went back to forty-five minutes. That seems to be the sweet spot for me.

After you've exercised your body, it's then time to exercise your mind.

BRAIN TRAINING

As we discussed in Chapter 1, too often we get so caught up in the daily pressures of our lives that we end up in operating mode. We lean on what we already know to get us through the day—to complete projects, to finish what we think others aren't capable of, to respond as quickly as we can to the latest client demand, to take care of our children and family, etc. Essentially these daily pressures will never end, and so we end up living our lives in operating mode. Again, it's definitely a way to survive, but it's not an effective strategy to thrive.

Brain training is a natural component of a healthy and constructive Creation Foundation because it allocates a time for us each day to reach beyond what we already know. Brain training forces us to expand our horizons, and with that expansion, increase our knowledge. And what you'll find, as I did, is once I started forcing myself to seek new information inputs, I became more curious about so many other things I hadn't even thought about before. Essentially, the process builds on itself. The more you start learning about new things, the more you want to learn about new things.

So how do you do it? I'm not presenting anything close to rocket science here. It's not complicated at all. Just choose a book about something you're interested in that's related in some way to your goals and dedicate time each day to actually reading it. This was revelatory to me because, as I told you, I was living my life in operating mode, running around each day trying to stave off some impending doom of failure. On top of that, I wasn't much of a reader, so the very last thing I would ever think to do is read a book every day. I was too busy for that! But I wasn't actually too busy. I just thought I was too busy, and I had no structure in my life to allow me to see how simple—and beneficial—this activity could be.

Setting a time for this is a little more difficult because everyone reads at different paces. But I think you should commit to reading ten to fifteen pages every day. The average person takes around two minutes to read a page, so this page range should put most people in the twenty-to-thirty-minute range. If you're a slower reader, start with ten pages; if you're a faster reader, start at fifteen. The important thing is to read!

And be sure to use this reading time to learn about something related to your goals. If you want to be a better parent, choose a book about parenting. If you want to open a new bakery in your town, choose a book about entrepreneurs or starting up a business. All of these steps in the Daily Five are to be channeling you toward your goals, so use this brain training time to expand your knowledge and curiosity in a way that will help you reach your ultimate destination.

WRITING IN THE DAILY LEDGER

This final step is of course the most important, but committing to the first four steps is crucial. Think of them as rungs in a ladder that help you elevate yourself to this final step in the Creation Foundation. Here you should commit to writing down your goals every day, twice a day. My suggestion is to do it once in the morning, as the final step in the Daily Five, and then once more before you go to sleep.

Many of my new clients scoff at this. They think it will be easy. But it's not. It's actually surprisingly difficult. That's why I have you do the first four steps. Writing your goals down each day takes commitment and, believe it or not, courage. You have to face your dreams, your successes, and your failures every single day. That's not an easy thing to do at all. It's much easier to distract ourselves with something that we deem important rather than evaluate where we might have fallen short on a given day, or are falling short over time, such as weeks or months. The Daily Ledger keeps you accountable 365 days a year. That's why it works.

But to just think you can snap your fingers and "do it" would be a mistake. You need to reshape your days to reshape your life. If you beat the sun up every morning, you already have a head start. You will then use that head start, that space in the day just for you, to reflect on your place in the universe and to build both your body and mind. Over time, that will strengthen your conviction and focus to write your goals in the Daily Ledger and the will to achieve the goals you set for yourself.

And just think…you will have accomplished all of this before most of America has even gotten out of bed.

CHAPTER 5

Step 2: Life Mapping

THERE'S A FAMOUS QUOTE FROM the writer and poet Maya Angelou that says, "You can't really know where you are going until you know where you have been." Nothing can be more true when it comes to changing your life and achieving all that you want in life.

We like to think of change as it happens in the movies. Suddenly there's some pivotal moment in the movie where everything just clicks for the character. They just decide then and there that everything is going to change. That's usually when the inspirational music comes on and there's a montage of all productive and constructive things our protagonist is doing to change their life and themselves: Suddenly the apartment is transformed from a complete mess to a spotless, super cool pad. Instead of watching TV, they are jogging along the river and working up a sweat at the gym. All the chips, cake, and beer get tossed in the garbage in favor of salad, fish, and mineral water. And suddenly at work, they're clicking on all cylinders to the surprise and clear admiration of their coworkers. It won't be long before our hero beats everyone at everything and walks off into the sunset rich in money and love, as the credits start to roll.

The thing is, if it was that easy to transform your life, everyone would do it! The truth is that change is hard. And because it's hard, it takes hard work. You have to be willing to be honest with yourself and take the time to really reflect on every detail of your life. This is where Life Mapping comes in.

I'm an accountant, so I look at everything very systematically. I can't tell you how many times a client of mine has come to me confused and distraught, saying, "I have no idea where all my money is going!" To me, there's only one way to solve this problem: I have my client scour their records to literally see where their money is going. They need to look at how they're spending their money not only on an annual or even a monthly level—that's too large of a time block to truly fix. No, the devil (in this case disappearing money) is in the details, and those details occur daily, not monthly or yearly.

I make my clients map out their spending habits for each and every day. What they find usually shocks them. They can't, for example, fathom how much money they are spending on lunch every day. Sometimes it's just what they're buying for themselves every day, but for my clients with small businesses, those "office lunch days" add up too. Likewise, morning coffee and donuts, buying bottled waters after hitting the gym, paying for gas and parking rather than taking public transportation, etc., are all smaller daily individual expenses, but collectively they add up—fast! Once my clients stop wondering where their money is going and actually take the time and do the hard work of figuring out where it's going on a daily basis, they can begin to make more cost-effective decisions. I call this Money Mapping, and it's the very first step in transforming personal and business budgets.

The funny thing is, when I have my clients do this, and they see the results, when they see clearly the way they're wasting money and ways they can stop doing that, they then wonder why they hadn't done this already. "This wasn't rocket science," they say to me— and I always totally agree. It's not. Money Mapping is actually a very easy and practical step to take to better manage your finances. That said, most people don't do it.

I've taken my strategy of Money Mapping in my accounting business and applied it here to transform people's entire lives. But this time instead of mapping money, I have them map time. Just as people wonder where all their money goes, they wonder where all their time goes. Here are some of the ways my clients express this to me. See if any of them sound familiar:

- "If I just had more time, I'd be able to achieve so much more!"

- "I'd love to do that, but unfortunately there's not enough time in my day."

- "I never stop working, and yet it seems like there's never enough time to get it all done."

- "There isn't enough time in the day for me to take on anything else."

- "Where does all the time go?"

- "I can't find the time to do anything that I actually want."

- "The time just flies by. Seems like it goes by faster every year."

If you're like most people—even well-organized people—you've probably expressed some version of this sentiment at some point in your life. It's natural.

Time *does* go by fast, and our chaotic modern world that's now dialed in 24/7 makes it go by even faster. In fact, some of our most modern "time-saving" technologies can end up being timewasters if you're not careful. But that's impossible to know unless you've done the hard work of finding out. Just as we need to account for our money, we need to account for our time. And so I have my clients do what I call Life Mapping.

Again, it's not enough to take an aerial view of how you spend your time. Monthly and even weekly reviews won't cut it. You have to get deep in the trenches here and look at every facet of your every day. That's the only way you can really understand how you spend your time—and how you're wasting it. In short, Life Mapping is the only way to accurately answer the question "Where does all my time go?"

LIFE MAPPING PROCESS

The Life Mapping process is simple but rigorous. You need to map out a full twenty-four hours of your day in thirty-minute increments—and you need to repeat this process for seven straight days. This will give you a full accounting of how your work week generally looks, as well as how your weekend looks, which, if you're in constant operating mode, might look very similar to your work week. In any case, you need to look beyond just a single twenty-four-hour segment or two because we all know each new day presents new challenges; each new day presents something different than the day before. So you need to look at a range of days to have a fuller sample to review that will help you understand how you're spending your time.

Don't get me wrong, plotting out what you do every thirty minutes for a week isn't easy, but nobody ever said transforming your life to reach your fullest potential and achieve your goals would be easy. But once complete, your Life Map will present you with a treasure trove of data to help you start reshaping how you think about time and your priorities in life. Think of your Life Map as a microscope that provides you with a magnified, super-detailed picture of your behavior—and, since your behavior also speaks to who you are as a person, you can think of your Life Map as a picture of yourself, of who you are.

The thirty-minute increments will ensure that you spare no activity in your day. There's nothing within that tight of a time span that you can overlook. Waking up, eating, exercising, working, parenting, driving, praying, reading, watching TV, browsing social media, whatever it is you're doing in any moment of any day should be noted in your Life Map. The more detailed the better. That means any activity that's exceeding a thirty-minute increment should be broken into finer detail. That applies even to something like sleep. Don't just block off six or seven hours for "sleep." Break those hours down into thirty-minute segments too. If you're literally sleeping straight through all those thirty-minute segments, great! But looking more closely with your Life Map, you might find that you're waking up at around the same time every night, or many nights, which might track to something you're doing during your day. Or you might find that you go to bed even later than you think are. (Sometimes time can get away from you when you're YouTubing in bed before you actually go to sleep!) That kind of late-night pattern might help explain your lethargy in the morning.

Be sure to do the same with what's likely going to take up another large block of your time: your typical workday. You should be noting *exactly* what it is that you're doing at work; it's not enough just to report "working" for eight straight hours. You need to know *what* you're doing at work at any given moment. That's when you really start to understand your behavioral patterns. And when you start to truly understand your behavioral patterns, you can begin to develop strategies to change and revise those patterns as needed.

Take my client Logan for example. He was a thirty-four-year-old who was just starting to have a family and wanted to start advancing at this job. But he just seemed to be treading water. It was understandable that he had more stress and obligations at home with his new baby, but he hadn't stopped working and yet seemed to never be able to generate new contacts or cultivate new clients—both of which would help him get noticed by his bosses and start to move up the ladder at this company. Logan was most definitely in operating mode.

Logan didn't get more than three days into his Life Mapping when he discovered a behavior that was absolutely sucking away a ton of his everyday time: emailing. He found that "emailing" was popping up five, six, sometimes seven times in a workday. It was not only a constant time-sucking activity, it was a constant distraction. When I asked him about this, he said, "You can't just write an email like you're texting a friend. I'm dealing with clients, sometimes clients with huge accounts. I had to think carefully about the wording I used, how exactly I said something, what exactly I should say, etc. Then I have to read it over, make sure I didn't spell something stupid. Basically, it takes up a lot of time and also a lot of mental energy…and I was doing that all day long!"

Ultimately, what Logan discovered wasn't that those emails weren't important; they of course were. He discovered that he lacked any ability to structure and prioritize his day. He was just constantly reacting to whatever came his way. In effect, by being in operating mode, he was inefficient and at the same time—and this was the true revelation for him—he was also devaluing himself. He felt that taking care of everyone else's business right there and then as soon as he found out about it was more important than his plans and goals.

It's tough to transform your life and achieve your full potential from the backseat. You need to be in the driver seat. Your Life Map will help you do that. So now Logan has a much more regimented time for emailing. He dedicates two blocks of time to read and respond to emails in a given workday: one hour in the morning (it's the final part of his beat the sun up ritual) and thirty minutes in the afternoon. The first session allows him to think more thoughtfully and respond more fully to clients about larger issues, and the second session allows him to address any smaller immediate items that might need addressing during the course of a day. Just this one small realization had profound benefits for Logan. "Much, much happier and more in control now," he told me. "Seeing that issue pop up in my Life Map and coming up with a plan to fix it went a long way in helping me get of operating mode and into a mindset that's helped me to take major steps in advancing my career goals in my company."

FIVE RULES OF LIFE MAPPING

By now you should understand the general process as well as the importance of Life Mapping to help transform your life and set you on a path to achieving your goals. But here are a few additional notes to keep in mind as you do so.

1. **Be honest**—about everything. This is your Life Map. So while sometimes it might not be pretty, it's still yours. You didn't start this process for a pat on the back for a job well done. You started this process to help you solve problems and better yourself. You can't do that without being honest about everything— that includes how you spend your days.

2. **Be brave**—being honest necessarily requires bravery. But just in case it's easier to be honest if you know you're also being brave, I put this in. Most people are afraid to look too closely at themselves in fear of what they might discover. It takes a fair dose of courage to take this plunge and to do so knowing that you're going to be completely open and honest about what you discover.

3. **Be selfish**—yes, you're doing this right now for yourself—and that's okay! And yes, you

will need a little extra time to get this all started. Micro-analyzing your days for a week straight might take you away from things you would ordinarily be doing, or people you might ordinarily be giving more attention to. Just be sure to communicate your intentions and goals clearly and honestly with your network of friends and loved ones.

4. **Be forgiving**—just because you're being honest with yourself doesn't mean you need to be mean to yourself. We all have flaws. We all have shortcomings. We all have ways of being unproductive or wasting time. That's life. Don't beat yourself up about something that you discover you're doing or not doing. The point of this exercise is to get everything out in the open so you can see it all clearly—and then begin the process of fixing it in a way that will be more helpful and constructive for you moving forward.

5. **Be resilient**—it's not easy to do this. You'll be surprised at how much it can take out of you over the course of a few days. But when you hit that wall, you need to have the resilience to keep going, to know that there's something important you might discover on day five,

six, or seven that wasn't apparent on day two, three, or four. Going that extra mile could very well be the one that pays off in the end. Hang in there!

CHAPTER 6

Step 3: Life Auditing

IF YOU READ THE FIRST few chapters, the title of this chapter shouldn't surprise you. I'm an accountant by trade, after all, and so I look at everything in terms of assets and liabilities. If you recall from earlier, an asset is something that you can consider beneficial to advancement in the future; an asset is a benefit to you and what you want to achieve. A liability, on the other hand, is the opposite. It's something you can consider an impediment to advancement in the future; a liability hinders or holds you back from what you want to achieve.

As an accountant, I typically look at assets and liabilities strictly in terms of dollars and sense. An aspect of a client's business that is consistently losing money and has little potential for growth would be considered a liability—that is, it's hurting the financial stability and future earnings potential of the business moving forward. Assets to a business are those aspects and investments that generate strong revenue that help the business grow. If a business hires a salesperson for $50,000 a year, and the salesperson generates $500,000 a year in revenue, that employee is clearly an asset to the company. My job as an accountant is to examine my clients' finances and determine what their assets and liabilities are. I do this through a formal process called an audit.

An audit might have a scary connotation for many people, as it's often referenced in terms of the IRS digging into your tax records (and trying to screw you out of your money!). And that is, in fact, an audit. But an audit isn't only something that the IRS does, and it doesn't have to be scary. Essentially an audit is just a very close inspection and analysis of data, and smart businesses run audits all the time. To ensure their finances are balanced, they might hire an outside accountant, someone like me, to conduct an external audit. To continually evaluate and improve the systems, processes, and strategies, businesses might run what's called an internal audit where managers collect and review a whole bunch of data to see what's working, what's not, and what they can do moving forward to get better and more efficient.

And it's this type of audit—an internal audit—that is similar to what we'll be doing with your Life Audit. What you did in Chapter 5 with your Life Mapping was to collect a large sample of data from your life. If you followed the guidelines I set out, you would have done the following:

↳ Logged what you were doing every thirty minutes for an entire day.

↳ Continued this exercise for seven straight days to get a full representation of how your life looks on both a work week and during the weekend.

↳ Been as specific as possible in terms of what you wrote down. That is, you would not just write down "working" but rather exactly what you were doing at work; you wouldn't just write down "relaxing" but rather exactly what you were doing when you were relaxing, etc.

↳ In engaging in this process, you would have tried as best as you could to adhere to the five rules of Life Mapping: be honest, brave, selfish, forgiving, and resilient.

If you were able to do all of these things for one week straight, you should have a pretty detailed idea of what the contours of your daily life look like. In effect, your Life Map now presents you with a bunch of important data about yourself that you need to now analyze through your Life Audit. Let's now walk through my three-step process for how you can conduct your Life Audit.

STEP 1: WRITE DOWN YOUR GOALS (AGAIN)

By this point, you will already have your goals written down in your Life Ledger, of course, but take this opportunity to write them down again as you begin your Life Audit. Keeping your goals fresh in your mind will help you better evaluate the data in front of you. Your goals should be what helps determine what you consider to be helpful or detrimental activities in your day. They serve kind of as a lens to view your activities and behavior through.

STEP 2: TAKE A BIRD'S EYE LOOK AT YOUR LIFE

If you have seven days of data in front of you, it might be a little intimidating. You might be asking, "Where the heck do I begin?" And that's totally normal! Having your life laid out in front of you for you to examine *is* intimidating. As I said in the last chapter, you have to be brave to engage in the process in the first place. But the old saying "You can't see the forest for the trees" applies here. When you're in the middle of something—in this case, your life—it's sometimes difficult to see the larger patterns that make up the bigger picture. Just like if you're in the middle of a forest, you might just see one tree after another, individually, unable to see the forest as a whole, the same thing happens to us in life: we just see one event or one behavior, individually, and can't ever put all these events and behaviors together to see the bigger picture of our life as a whole.

So, now that we have your life plotted out in thirty-minute increments, go through and analyze each event using the following code:

℞ Highlight anything you're happy about, that you view as a positive, in green (or whatever color makes you happy).

℞ Highlight anything that you find annoying or disappointing—basically, anything you find more negative that you wish you weren't doing—in red (or again, whatever color makes you unhappy).

℞ Highlight anything you're not quite sure about in a neutral color.

For this activity, I typically suggest my clients do this on hard copy printed paper, or at least print it out after they've color-coded everything. This way, they can lay out all the data on the floor and start seeing in one sweeping view—like a bird flying overhead—the different colors and any patterns that might be forming when looked at all at once. Think of it as an opportunity to get out of the thick, dense forest of your life and instead hop in a hot air balloon and slowly drift above it all.

Just as that forest would look different if you're flying above rather than hiking through it, so should your life when looking at it plotted out in your Life Map. Spend some time with it. Absorb what you see. All the information and insight you can get from this will be useful, be it positive or negative.

Are there hours in the day or days in your week that are popping out in one particular color or another? A large swath of green on a certain day might start to serve as a model for your goals moving forward. On the other hand, a consistent pattern of red might be an indication of something you need to either remedy or avoid altogether. You might also see reds and greens leapfrogging each other every day. This could be an indication that your life is currently without structure.

While that might not be what you want to learn, it might be exactly what you need to learn. You can't fix what you don't know is broken! So, again, be forgiving of yourself. Don't get down on yourself if you don't like the patterns that are appearing to you. Now that you can identify what might not be working, you're in a vastly better position to change it! And you will!

I suggest not trying to do this exercise all at once. It takes time to reflect and absorb this much information and really think through your behaviors and your life. I remember when I first did this, I was seeing a LOT of red, and much of that red was labeled "Drinking." Was this something I was proud of? Of course not. I was embarrassed. I was ashamed. And I wanted to just toss it all in the garbage, burn it, just get rid of it so I didn't have to see it anymore—all the things that weren't going right in my life. But I didn't. I actually had my Life Map out in my living room for weeks, which forced me to keep looking at it, thinking about it, thinking about my life. Over time, I've decided it was the best thing I could've done. It was like literally facing my demons. After a while, I went from embarrassed and disappointed to angry and resolute. I became determined to change, to fix it all, to be the person I knew I was and wanted to be. And I did. But you have to stick with it.

So, for this step, just keep this in mind: Stick with it. Don't shy away from it. Absorb the data, engage with it, because it will ultimately be what moves you to the next level.

STEP 3: CREATING LIFE ASSETS AND LIABILITIES

Once you've spent some time absorbing your Life Map, it's time for the next step in your Life Audit: officially breaking down your time into assets and liabilities.

The first part of this should be relatively easy if you've worked through Step 2 in earnest. That is, if you coded what you felt were positive and negative activities in your life, these would typically map to one column or the other. For example, if your goal is growing your client base by 50 percent in the next year, and there are time segments during your week that you dedicate to networking or reaching out to new potential customers, that would likely be highlighted in green and get moved into the asset column. Similarly, if you find that most days you're spending an hour or two lying in bed watching YouTube videos before starting your day, you'd probably have that activity highlighted in red and naturally move it to the liability column (unless, of course, being up to date on funny cat videos is a strategy for client growth).

Ultimately, this step is where we merge Steps 1 and 2 together. Step 1 had you reconfirm your goals in writing. Step 2 had you color-code your Life Map into positive, negative, and neutral behaviors and activities. In this third step, you should check your coding against your goals before finally designating each as either an asset or liability. If you feel the activity or behavior is a way to help you advance and achieve your goals, then you should designate it as an asset. If you feel that the activity or behavior is in fact a hindrance or an obstacle to achieving your stated goals, then move it to the liability column.

Starting with the ones you coded as either positive or negative on your Life Map will make getting started on this process easier. It will also help you continue to formulate and refine the ways in which you can start achieving your goals.

When you've designated all your positives and negatives, you can then move on to the more ambiguous aspects of your Life Map—those segments of time you originally highlighted as neutral or that you were unsure about. Ideally, having spent so much time absorbing your coded Life Map and then spending time in this current step designating your activities and behaviors as either assets or liabilities, the parts of your life that might originally have been more ambiguous in terms of their relevance and utility might be more clear to you now—that is, it might be obvious to you whether they can help you achieve your goals as an asset or hinder your progress and are a liability. It's likely, though, that some of these "gray" parts of your life will remain unclear to you, so let's take a minute or two to think through these challenging aspects of your Life Map.

Take sleep, for example. It's not as if we're setting the world on fire with our brilliance when we're tucked under the covers and dreaming at night. Yet, without proper sleep, we will be far less productive than we would ordinarily be. So sleep is essential to everyone—the question is, how much sleep? Most sleep research will claim a range of seven to eight hours of sleep is what most healthy adults should be getting each night. But we all know there are some people who seem to be able to function very well on less sleep, while there are others who definitely veer toward needing maybe a few more winks each night if they are going to be happy and productive during the waking hours. You might be struggling with that sleep-wake line, and so it comes down to knowing yourself. Would getting an extra hour of sleep each night help you to be more productive? If so, that would make it an asset (at least for now—you can always go back and change it later). Or would getting that extra hour of sleep really just be laziness on your part? If your honest appraisal is yes, then move it to the liability column.

What about something like checking social media? As we discussed in Chapter 1, that depends on what your goals are, too, as well as how often you check it, when you check it, what exactly you're checking, etc.

Basically, as with everything in your Life Map and Life Audit, it requires you truly looking deeply into what your goals are and what you need to do to get there. You need some down time, too, to just relax and decompress. For many people, especially now that many more people work from home, that line between work and leisure, luxury and necessity, can be tricky to navigate. Social media, for example, is vital to many businesses and entrepreneurs today, but it's also a huge timewaster at the same time. I put social media in my asset list, but I schedule it during my day so that I will use it as constructively as possible. Rather than lying in bed for an extra hour at night before I go to sleep scrolling through social media feeds, as I once used to do all the time, I have calendar blocked a time to look at social media in my day where I'm not as susceptible to using it to procrastinate or distract me from the other asset activities that would help advance me toward my goals. It's worked great for me. If you're honest with yourself, you'll be able to strike the right balance too.

There are other potential vices, too, like extravagant lunches or dinners, binging TV shows and movies, perhaps having drinks to unwind sometimes. It would be foolish to think you can go through life without having any fun or any guilty pleasures. That's not reasonable. It's probably not healthy either. But if you're in control of every aspect of your day, you can block these activities so that they're stitched into the overall structure of your day; you can turn your vices into assets—but you have to be intentional about it. You have to be mindful of what you're doing, when you're doing it, and why you're doing it.

That's a lot to bear all the time, every day, but this is why once you get going, your Life Ledger is so vital, so important to keep you focused, on track, and committed to your goals. It reaffirms daily what you want and why you want it. If you don't have that constant affirmation, it's very easy to lose sight of your initial plan, or even the reasons you made the plan in the first place. The Life Ledger doesn't allow you to do that. It makes you recommit each and every day, which brings you closer to who you want to be and what you want out of life, each and every day.

CHAPTER 7

Step 4: The Filter: Creating an Asset-Only Life

Let's review all that you've done so far in your Life Ledger journey. You've started brainstorming your Creation Foundation. You've taken the time to Life Map a full week of your life, breaking down every aspect of your day into thirty-minute segments. You've then done a full Life Audit, where you designate each of your daily behaviors and activities as either an asset or a liability. The question now is: What do you do with this list?

This chapter starts to put all of this careful examination you've done into action. You will begin to transform your every day to transform your life.

But let's be clear. This is not easy! Doing something once a year, no problem. Doing something once a month, pretty simple. Doing something even once a week, yeah, shouldn't be too hard. But doing something every day? That takes commitment. That takes conviction. And it also takes a plan.

Your Life Ledger is that plan.

MAXIMIZING YOUR ASSETS

What we ultimately want to do now is to fill your days with asset activities and get rid of all your liability activities. We filter these activities through the goals you've created for yourself in your Life Ledger. If the activity is beneficial in some way to helping you achieve the goals in your Life Ledger, then it becomes part of your daily asset activities. At the end of the day (literally and figuratively), all your activities and behaviors in your asset list should help you advance toward your goals. You have to be brutal with yourself about this, but the payoff is huge. Imagine—every day of your life spent in the betterment of yourself, propelling you further, higher, and to more success than you ever imagined before. This is the inevitable outcome of transforming your days with only activities that will benefit you in the long run. An assets-only life.

This is why your Creation Foundation is so important as you start in on this process. The activities I outlined for you in Chapter 4 will serve as the basic building blocks to get you in the practice of bettering yourself and making your days more productive through asset activities.

- ♫ Beating the Sun up—gives you a head start each and every day to doing what best helps you achieve your goals.

- ♫ Morning Meditation—helps you gain and retain perspective on where you are in your life, what's important to you, and where you want to go in the future.

- ♫ Exercising—makes your stronger physically, which will ultimately also help you get stronger mentally.

- ♫ Brain Training—keeps you advancing your depth of knowledge related to your goals. Lifelong learning cultivates the mind and soul, which contributes to success and fulfillment.

- ♫ Writing in the Daily Ledger—keeps you convicted and focused each and every day about what you want out of life and what you need to attain it.

With these as your foundational asset building blocks, you will then start to schedule your day with only your asset activities. As you did with your Life Map, plot out your schedule in thirty-minute increments. It doesn't mean you can only do something for thirty minutes at a time. If there's a really important asset activity that consumes multiple, or many, thirty-minute segments, that's totally fine! Great, actually. But breaking down your day into such fine detail will help you stay focused on what's most important and help ensure that you're not wasting any time that could be better spent working toward your goals in some way.

When we think in large blocks of time, we have a tendency to build in more slack and down time. That's just human nature. For example, if you say, "This morning, I'm going to do X, Y, and Z," it's not at all clear precisely when those X, Y, and Z activities are going to get done. Is X going to start at 6:00 in the morning? 8:00 in the morning? 10:00? And where do Y and Z fit around that? And how long will it take you to do each one? You can already see such a loose time block actually prompts more questions than answers when you look at it logistically—which is how you need to look at everything as you reshape your life to achieve your goals. So mapping out your day in a granular way—for us, thirty-minute segments—answers those questions through the scheduling process. Our thirty-minute segments will make very clear what you are doing and when.

- 6:30—Activity X
- 7:00—Activity X
- 7:30—Activity X
- 8:00—Activity Y
- 8:30—Activity Y
- 9:00—Activity Z
- 9:30—Activity Z
- 10:00—Activity Z
- 10:30—Activity Z

Every minute of your day will be accounted for, leaving yourself fewer questions, less guesswork, and more time to be productive.

Here's the thing: if you're like most people (myself included), you likely had a decent amount of your time previously being taken up by liabilities. When I first created my asset-only daily schedule, I was in short order confronted by a huge amount of empty thirty-minute time slots. My days had become so consumed with liability activities that when I took them out of the equation, I wasn't at all sure what I was going to do with myself each day.

But of course, this is part of the process of redis-covering your life. This is the absolute best problem to have. Because you've been following the Life Ledger process, because you have worked so hard to map out and audit your life, because you have been honest with yourself about what's working and what's not, you have essentially answered the question so many millions of people ask themselves everyday: "Where does all my time go?" You now have the answer! Your time was sucked away by far too many time-wasting, unproduc-tive liability activities! Your process of self-discovery through the Life Ledger is showing you that far from having too few hours in the day, you actually have too many! It's a luxury we all wish for but few achieve—but you just have.

Those empty white spaces in your asset-only sched-ule are ripe with possibility. Let's call them open spaces of opportunity. You've created for yourself opportuni-ties for growth that you can implement every day. This is a regenerative process, meaning that you can brain-storm new ideas, new strategies, and new ways to reach your goals, and those new ideas and strategies give birth to even more ideas and more strategies. Many of my cli-ents even double down on this process and schedule a segment of time each day just to creatively brainstorm ways to innovate to produce more opportunities and strategies for success. You'll be amazed at just how creative you can be once you give yourself the time and space to do so.

And to be clear, you're not going to get your schedule right the first time around. This is a process of discovery and creation. Failure is part of that process. We discover what works by discovering what doesn't. Just as you did with your Life Audit, go easy on yourself when ideas don't quite work out as planned. So you might be asking, how will I know if something it working or not? Great question! This is where your goals come in.

Your goals serve as the filter for all your assets. If you recall from our earlier discussions, we have your goals, and then we have your DTs, your Daily Targets. Your activities should be helping you to productively hit those DTs, which help get you closer to your goals. This is something you constantly will be assessing and reassessing through your Life Ledger.

For example, let's say you set a goal for yourself to increase your income by $100,000 a year. Sounds great. But how are you going to do that? $100,000 isn't just going to drop from the sky. You have to go out there and make it happen. And it's not going to happen all at once. It will have to happen through the course of business, which happens not once a year (which is your overall goal), it happens monthly, weekly, daily. So let's say you start breaking it down into smaller, more manageable segments. Say, to get to $100,000 by the end of the year, you need to roughly make $10,000 more every month. $10,000 times twelve months gets you to $120,000. Then, after taxes (if you want to take it to that level), you're pretty much at your goal.

But we don't accomplish things by the month either. We achieve success and reach our goals by what we set out for ourselves every day. This is where your DTs come in. This is where your asset schedule comes in. What DTs are you going to set for yourself each day, and what activities are you going to integrate into your day that help you hit those targets? Maybe it's spending thirty minutes every day making cold calls to potential customers. Maybe it's spending one hour every day going the extra mile for an existing client who you think might be able to open up opportunities in the future. Maybe it's spending one hour a day doing community outreach, getting to know local businesspeople and entrepreneurs. Obviously not all of these activities are going to pay off right away. Reaching your goals takes time. But as you recommit every day to your goals by writing them down in your Life Ledger, you will absolutely start to understand what activities are constructive and productive—either short term, long term, or both—and which ones are missing the mark. If one activity or another is missing the mark, it's no longer an asset activity. And if it's not an asset activity, then it becomes a liability. It's not helping you achieve what you want, and so it must be removed from your daily schedule and replaced with something that will, or potentially will.

And so it will continue this way—you filtering your asset activities through your Life Ledger goals, revising, refining, and reinventing as you go.

As challenging as this process can be in the beginning, rest assured, the longer you do this, the more natural it will become for you. A life of discovery and creation will become part of who you are—and consequently, a life dedicated to your goals will see you achieve them—and then set new goals for yourself.

CONTROLLING YOUR LIABILITIES

There is a hitch, though, and it's one that you absolutely need to be mindful of. Those sneaky little liabilities that you got rid of? They don't just go away that easily. That's what made them liabilities, and that's what will continue to make them liabilities, if you let them. Bad habits are the hardest to break, and so it will take more than identifying them to get them out of your life for good. In order to maximize your assets, you need to make sure that your liabilities don't creep back into your schedule or your life. Let's look at a couple of ways of doing this.

One way I've had clients take control of their liabilities is to do just that: control your liabilities, don't let your liabilities control you. To control anything in life, you need to confront whatever it is head on. We can't avoid our weaknesses. We can't hide from them and pretend they're not there. That never works. Your liabilities will always catch up with you. I know this all too well.

For the longest time, I kept trying to pretend that my drinking wasn't a problem. I would pretend it didn't control me. I would play mind games with myself to kind of trick myself into thinking everything was okay, that I had it under control. If I only drink beer, I'd tell myself, then it's not a problem; people with real drinking problems drink hard alcohol, like vodka or whiskey. Or I'd say as long as I can keep doing my job and am productive at work, I don't have a problem; people with real drinking problems are too hungover to do their jobs effectively. I'd go on and on like this, setting up all these different rationales for why I did not have a problem. In fact, coming up with reasons that I didn't have a problem became an additional liability by itself. My mind became preoccupied with denying I had a problem at all!

In effect, this denial was me hiding from the truth, hiding from my reality. And I wasn't able to start controlling my drinking until I was able to admit that I couldn't control it—that it was controlling me. I couldn't fix it until I owned up to it. It may sound a bit strange, but my life started to change for the better, the day I could actually write down on a piece of paper the following: "I have a drinking problem. I am an alcoholic." That may seem like the easiest thing in the world to do, but for me, it was so incredibly difficult. I knew for the longest time that I did have a problem, but I wouldn't admit it to myself. And so the truth was in me all along, kind of trapped inside my head—haunting me. To finally write it down, so I could see it—and other people could see it—outside of myself was life altering. It was like I exorcised a demon. I was finally brave enough to admit it and have it written out in black and white for anyone to see. It was that day that I started to take control of my biggest liability and transform my life to what I wanted it to be, to who I wanted to be in it.

Of course, this wasn't my only liability. I had lots more! (Yes, I was a mess!) But I did with those what I did with my drinking: I wrote them all down. But I didn't just write them down once and call it a day. I wrote them down and then printed them out in multiple versions and put them all around me so I would constantly be reminded of what my liabilities were, which would remind me of what I did not want to go back to. It was my way of owning my liabilities. I put a copy on the refrigerator door; I put a copy on my desk at work; I put a copy on my desk at home. I put them anywhere I thought I would be able to see them at least once a day to remind myself that these are the behaviors and activities that are weaknesses of mine and that I need to avoid if I want to achieve my goals. And when they would start to blend into the woodwork, so to speak, as everything does over time, I would move them. I'd either put a copy in a new place on my desk or I'd put a copy in a new place entirely. Whatever I had to do to keep reminding myself of what my liabilities were, which gave me the conviction to renounce them and pursue my assets instead. It was my way of owning and controlling what for far too long had controlled me.

And it's worked for my clients too. One of my clients thought I was crazy at first when I told her to do this. I could see her staring at me skeptically as I told her to write down her liabilities and put them all over her apartment, inside her car, etc. But she did, and it didn't take long at all before she called to tell me how empowering it was for her. And it can be for you too.

My suggestion is that you write your liabilities out in a series of "I statements." This allows you to fully commit to owning your bad habits, qualities, and characteristics about yourself that could be holding you back. I statements are simply sentences that start with "I."

> ↳ I have a drinking problem. I am an alcoholic.

> ↳ I watch way too much television at night.

> ↳ I have no discipline when it comes to putting other people's priorities above my own.

> ↳ I lack time management skills.

> ↳ I constantly procrastinate.

> ↳ I have not been as good of a spouse as I should be.

> ↳ I am afraid of failing.

> ↳ I always feel the need to be nice and apologize when things go wrong, even when it's not my fault.

> ↳ I avoid conflict in ways that sometimes undermine my own best interests.

> ↳ I spend too much money on things.

> ↳ Etc.

Ultimately, what these I statements do is make you more accountable. When we stow our thoughts, fears, and weaknesses away in the recesses of our mind, we are trying not to account for them. We are trying to avoid accountability. But by airing them out in the light of day, by confronting them in a form outside of ourselves, we are forced to acknowledge, confront, and overcome them.

Sometimes it's helpful to think about things in reverse. So think back to when you were a kid. If you got a good grade at school, you probably were very proud if your parents put it up on the refrigerator door for everyone to see. You might even point to it for visiting family and friends, as if to say, "Look what I'm capable of!" In all likelihood, if you earned any trophies or awards for sports and clubs you belonged to, you'd do something similar: put it on display on your bedroom wall or a shelf in your room. We all do this. We want people to see the positives in us. It helps reinforce who we are, who we want to be, and what we're capable of. It's also the exact reason that we don't hang up the F's we received in school or print out the competition standings where we came in last. When we aren't doing what we feel we're capable of, we often try to cover it up. We like to take accountability for the things we like and avoid the things we don't.

But when those weaknesses start to slowly erode who we are and who we want to be, the only way to fix it is to take control over it. The only person who's going to fix you, after all, is you. Displaying your weaknesses and keeping them top of mind—that is, being account-able for them at all times—will go a long way in help-ing you to control your liabilities so you can maximize your assets.

And it's this principle of accountability that's at the root of the second strategy. Just as it's helpful to make yourself accountable for your liabilities, it's also help-ful to have a partner in this endeavor. I call this person your Accountability Partner.

Your Accountability Partner is someone who you can truly trust in life to be honest with you, even when honesty will be difficult and maybe uncomfortable. But to that same end, your Accountability Partner is some-one who you know loves you, who supports you, who has your back. This person could be a family member—an aunt, uncle, or sibling—a close friend, your boyfriend, girlfriend, or spouse. Some people prefer to hire a pro-fessional outside of their inner social network, such as a counselor or business or life coach. Whoever it is, their role will always be the same: your Accountability Partner is someone who knows your liabilities, knows what you struggle with, and is someone who will share in the challenge of helping you to control those liabili-ties—by holding you accountable for your actions and sticking to your asset-only life.

The way in which your Accountability Partner will serve in this role depends on lots of things—your personality and what you need; your relationship with this person outside of this role in your life (your dynamic with a spouse, for example, will surely be different than with a professional business coach or your favorite aunt); and what stage in your transformation process you're in (what you will need when just starting your Life Ledger will be different than what you need after two years of evolving in this process). I tell my clients to do what feels most natural. If you need someone to call you so you can give them status updates, great. If you need face-to-face accountability, that works too. You might feel at first you need a daily check-in, and then that pace might slow over time to weekly or even monthly check-ins. And of course, if you feel your resolve slipping, you might want to increase this number accordingly.

As you can see, flexibility is key. What matters most is that you have someone who knows what your liabilities are and has a stake in seeing that you remain in control of them. You know then that you won't be just letting yourself down, you'll be letting your Accountability Partner now down too. That can be a powerful motivation in and of itself. It all starts with you, of course. Again, only you can fix you. But having a sounding board outside of yourself, someone you know and trust to be accountable to as well, can be helpful.

My clients always end up asking me, which should I do, I statements or Accountability Partner? But I feel this is a personal question that you have to answer for yourself based on who you are, what your personality is like, what your situation is like. Be true to yourself. For me, I started with I statements and eventually brought on an Accountability Partner—but not because I was struggling, but rather because I was starting to thrive. I brought on an Accountability Partner to help get me to the next higher level. But some people might feel an Accountability Partner is, first and foremost, what they need just to get started. And that's fine. Again, we're all different. What's important is that you're imposing accountability on yourself to control your liabilities and maximize your assets.

CHAPTER 8

Step 5: Outsource to Elevate

So I NEED YOU TO bear with me here. For an entire chapter we just discussed the importance of accountability, how important accountability is to maximizing your assets and controlling your liabilities. Now in this chapter, it might seem like I'm contradicting all that—but I want you to know up front that I'm not. Personal accountability is absolutely critical to transforming your life and achieving your goals. But in order to reach your fullest potential, in order to reach the greatest heights, you have to let go of some of the tasks and responsibilities that might get you to one level but not the next. Ultimately, once you really are fully immersed in your Life Ledger process, you need to know how to outsource.

The ability to outsource is what allows you to truly elevate—but it's not necessarily intuitive. For many people—people who are really dedicated and hardworking, like you—outsourcing can be really scary. So let's talk about how all this works.

One way or another, you have probably heard of "outsourcing." You have heard it used in terms of sending jobs overseas—that is, outsourcing American jobs—but that's not at all what I'm talking about here. Outsourcing in the framework of the Life Ledger is to delegate responsibilities and tasks that you don't necessarily need to be doing anymore. In effect, outsourcing is delegating tasks to others so that you can free up your time to do things that only you can do and that are important to achieving your goals.

But outsourcing tasks can be anxiety-inducing, if not downright scary. And it can be scary for the precise reason that you are such a responsible, hardworking person. If you didn't care about what you did, you wouldn't have any fear at all—because you wouldn't care! For people who lack responsibility and dedication, outsourcing is ideal. (Outsource everything!) But when you care about your work, when you care about your roles in life, when you care about the quality and effectiveness of outcomes, you tend to want to do it all yourself.

On one hand, this is a great quality. It's in many ways worked to bring you where you are in your life today. But on the other hand, your need to do everything yourself might be the biggest obstacle holding you back from reaching your fullest potential. Why? Because you can't do it all and have it all at the same time. Believe me, I've tried. It doesn't work. What it ends in is endless operating and, finally, burnout.

Much of this challenge comes from how we're raised. Most of us have been raised with an "insourcing" mentality. To do everything ourselves, to be independent and not need anyone else's help. As you grow up, insourcing is what we learn. We finally move out of our parents' house and learn to do our own laundry, do our own shopping, make our own meals. Then we have to find a job to pay our own bills, and we try to do that job as effectively as we can, with as little help from colleagues and managers as possible. Intuitively, that just makes sense. And, in many ways, it does make sense— so long as you're not trying to constantly achieve greater things, bigger things.

Most of us are so accustomed to insourcing that we need to learn how to outsource. I think of it as a muscle that needs to be trained. We need to train our outsourcing muscle. And if you're talented and smart, it's a muscle that you may never have worked out before because, if you're like me, you always have the mindset that nobody else is going to do something quite as good as you would do it—so you might as well do it yourself. And this applies in most any context.

Let's say you're a mom whose primary work right now is raising her children but who's also looking to start up a small business making gourmet cupcakes that are absolutely adored by family, friends, and neighbors. There are few jobs as demanding as being a mom and raising a family, and so the question invariably will arise: I'd love to, but where do I find the time? There aren't enough hours in the day to take care of my family and start a business!

Most moms who I've known, including my own mom and my wife, are amazing with their family. They do anything and everything for them, and so feeling like there's not enough hours in the day makes complete sense. But that's when you have to reset. That's when the Life Ledger can help. And if this mom has gone through all of the steps we've discussed in this book, she will come to a point where outsourcing will be necessary in order to elevate and move to the next level of starting a business in earnest. So she has to overcome that insourcing mindset of feeling the need to do everything herself and figure out what activities in her day could potentially be outsourced.

If you're a mom with two or three kids, laundry might be a time-consuming activity each week. It's something that absolutely needs to get done, but mom would have to ask herself: am I the only person who could sufficiently do this job? If the answer is no, the next question is, how can I outsource it? Perhaps an older child can take on this task every week as part of their chore list. Is there a housekeeper who is already being paid to do some cleaning around the house? Are there cost-efficient laundry services in the area? Is there some way to trade off services with another mom in the neighborhood? Outsourcing the laundry could alone save this mom upward of eight to ten hours each week.

And the thing is, once you start exercising the outsourcing muscle, it gets stronger and stronger, and it becomes easier and more intuitive to start outsourcing other tasks. As important as it is to many moms to be there for their children, is it essential that every spare hour of their day is spent watching, caring for, and being with their children? Might it be possible to outsource an hour or so after nap time or a couple of hours after the kids get home from school to have a babysitter or mother's helper be in charge a few days a week? Add four or five hours of outsourced playtime each week to the eight to ten hours of outsourced laundry, and this mom suddenly has carved out two additional workdays to work on her business each week.

And there's a compounding effect with outsourcing. Not only do you become better at delegating, but the people you entrust with these responsibilities often become more efficient and skilled as well, which allows them to take on more responsibility, which allows you to outsource more tasks, which frees up more time for you to achieve more important goals that only you can do.

I experienced this myself just recently with a new business I was starting. Obviously for a new business, getting your name and brand out there on social media to start building connections, name recognition, and community relationships is huge. And although I should know better by now, I reverted back to my old insourcing ways. For the first few months, I was on social media constantly. Checking hit rates, visits, responding to posts, monitoring traffic and comments, etc. I didn't really realize how much time I was spending on this aspect of the business until I found myself in the office, in the dark, and it was almost midnight when my wife called, totally worried. She asked me, "Where are you? What are you doing?" And I was like, yeah, what am I doing?

The next day, I came into the office and called in Meg, one of our new admins. She was fresh out of college, was a marketing major, grew up on social media, and was clearly hardworking and eager for opportunities. Outsourcing this to her was a no-brainer, and I was an idiot for not having thought to do it sooner. And as soon as I did—almost immediately—I could feel a sense of relief. I felt like a weight had been lifted. I had fallen into operating mode without even knowing it, and outsourcing just this one task made me realize it. It didn't take Meg long to rise to the occasion. She was great at managing the social media for this start-up, far better than I was. And so it was what I call a 360 win. Meg won by gaining valuable work experience. I won by freeing myself to do higher-level strategy planning and implementation, and the business won by Meg and I both utilizing our time more efficiently and effectively to grow our client base and increase revenue.

In both of these cases—the mom wanting to start her own business and me trying to ramp up a new start-up—outsourcing is critical to taking it to the next level. In both cases outsourcing would be the key to elevating. In strictly business terms, outsourcing is essential to scaling—that is, growing one's business. I like to use the term elevating because, as you know, the Life Ledger doesn't just have to be used for business purposes, it can help you achieve whatever you want in life.

When you're first looking for activities to outsource, it can be confusing because many of the activities you're currently doing are important. Like, doing the laundry is an important task, especially when you're raising a family. Social media is now vital to a start-up. But just because it's important doesn't mean that you have to be doing it. You need to be able to make this distinction because sometimes the importance of these activities serves as excuses not to outsource—that is, because you can rationalize and explain their importance, you legitimize your need to retain direct control over them. So that's why I call activities that are important but not necessary for you to be doing Indirect Asset Activities.

One of my clients, Logan, for example, was trying to elevate this business, trying to get it to the next level by developing a larger book of business. He didn't have the time to do all the things he needed to do to accomplish this goal. And the list to grow a business can be quite long and daunting, filled with important activities but not necessary for Logan to have to do. Like scheduling. Scheduling is an indirect asset activity. Sending proposals, Indirect Asset Activity. Essentially, anything that you can train somebody else to do is an Indirect Asset Activity. We know that they help us reach our goals, but it's not something that we should be directly related to. We should instead be directly related to the training of that individual or training on that actual activity, but not directly involved in doing it ourselves.

We cannot scale, we cannot elevate, when we're directly involved in those types of Indirect Asset Activities. If we are, they end up becoming operating liabilities that inhibit growth. They become obstacles that keep us down and prevent us from reaching our full potential.

And let's be clear, outsourcing will feel like work at first. As you train that muscle, it's kind of tiring, because you're stressed and you'll doubt yourself. You'll start questioning yourself: Will this person be able to do what's needed? Will they mess it up? Am I doing the right thing? Am I creating more work for myself? What if something goes wrong?...And this is all natural. Being anxious about anything new is natural, as we've discussed throughout this book, but outsourcing is essential to elevating. It really is. And so let's stop and think about what good comes from this.

The goal of outsourcing is, as we've said, to elevate—or for a business to scale. Now pause here and think about what this means—to elevate and scale. It's a life without limits. It's a life that opens up new pathways and opportunities for growth. A life unfettered by tasks best done by someone else is a life that allows you the space and freedom to cultivate your best self in an effort to elevate and reach greater and greater heights. This is the life you've always wanted, and this is the final step in achieving it.

One of my other clients, Paul, has made it his goal to outsource everything. He now outsources entire businesses, which has allowed him to create a mini empire. He comes up with a business idea now, lays out a strategy, and outsources the rest to the people he trusts the most—and he trusts them because they've all done it all before. This is part of the compounding process. It's not as if Paul started with multiple businesses. It's not as if Paul was always outsourcing. He had to start small, with outsourcing one task, and then another, and another. He found people who could do the task, often better than he might've done it himself. The more they learned, the more they could handle, and the more this freed Paul to take on bigger and bolder projects. His goal now is to continue to do just this: outsource to elevate.

And if you're still skeptical, if you're still nervous or afraid to outsource once you put this book down and start getting to the actual nitty gritty of beginning to outsource, remember this: nobody is self-made. I honestly don't believe that's possible. We all need other people. We rely on others every day, often without even knowing it. We rely on bus drivers and Uber drivers to pick us up on time to take us where we need to go. We rely on sanitation workers to do the hard work of ensuring our waste is removed every week to keep our neighborhoods free of germs and disease. We rely on police officers to keep us safe in our towns and on our highways and streets. If we were constantly having to perform these and so many other tasks all the time, we wouldn't be able to innovate and find new and better ways of doing things. We outsource so many of our daily operations without even knowing it.

And when we think of the world's most innovative and successful people, we should also remember they, too, didn't do it by themselves. Bill Gates, Oprah Winfrey, Jeff Bezos, Martha Stewart—all of these now household names needed to outsource, rely on, and trust hundreds, if not thousands, of people along their journeys. Even now, they rely on all their managers, accounting teams, strategists, factory workers, etc., to keep these businesses functioning at the highest level. They all needed, and still need, to outsource to elevate.

I personally try to follow the advice of yet another groundbreaking, innovative entrepreneur: Richard Branson. Branson's names and companies are recognized around the world today, but this wasn't always the case. As a kid, he had difficulty in school and suffered from dyslexia, but he didn't let that stop him. He instead started innovating and creating as soon as he possibly could. He tried to start up a Christmas tree company when he was just a little kid, thinking he could grow them and sell them himself. As you might imagine, this early endeavor didn't work out too great, but he didn't let that stop him. He immediately got back on the horse and successfully launched a magazine—by the age of sixteen.

He went on to build an empire. His umbrella company, called Virgin, grew from his highly successful record company to an international airline to a hotel chain. He recently flew to space in yet another one of his companies, Virgin Galactic. But none of this would be possible without his ability to outsource. One person alone can't create multiple world-renowned business empires without an extraordinary amount of help along the way. But you can't get that help if you don't outsource. Branson is a master at outsourcing to elevate.

He has five simple rules he follows, which he discusses in the context of business, but it could apply to any endeavor, big or small, personal or professional.

The first one is what you might expect: know your strengths and weaknesses. This is what I've been telling you all along, from the X Factor through the entire Life Ledger process. All of it is dependent upon you knowing what you're good at, but even more importantly, knowing what you're not good at, what you need to improve on or very possibly what you need to outsource.

The second of Branson's rules is to assess the strengths and weaknesses of your team. In business, this is obviously the people you're working with and oftentimes the people subordinate to you. You need to understand what each person on your team excels at so you can put them in positions to succeed. If you don't have a good feel for what your colleagues or employees can and can't do, you might set them up for failure, which of course then sets yourself up for failure. So knowledge of your team is critical. If you put someone in a position they're not suited for, it will have a negative cascading effect. They will lose confidence in themselves, which then reduces their motivation and productivity, which then ultimately hurts the business. And if you're outsourcing and seeing negative results, you might lose confidence in your ability to outsource well or, worse, the need to outsource anything at all. This would be the absolute worse consequence because then you might revert back to trying to do everything yourself—which then might mean you go back into operating mode.

But this second rule is important beyond just business. It's important in relationships too. Think about how you are with your loved ones, your kids. You always want to know the strengths and weaknesses of those around you, so that you can set them up for the best possible chance for success.

Rule three is based on rule two. Branson stresses the need to bring in people and move people around depending on the weaknesses you see in your team— and in yourself. It's useful to go back to the example of the mom needing to free up time to start her new business. If she needs to outsource some of the daily and weekly household chores, she will need to assess the strengths and weaknesses of her immediate family members. Can they handle the dishwashing duties? Will they be able to clean well enough? Are they old enough to take care of the laundry? Do they have enough time in their own personal schedules to handle additional duties without having a negative effect on their other obligations? If the answer to any of these questions is "no," then she might have to bring in outside help to offset the weaknesses she's detected in her immediate family team. If she's not able to adapt and adjust based on her assessments, then she won't have the time to start up her business and achieve her goals.

Branson also stresses the importance in creating a safe environment and culture when outsourcing. You can't delegate responsibility to others and instill fear in them at the same time. You need to make sure everyone knows that mistakes will happen, that their opinions matter and are valuable, and that they all should feel empowered to voice their opinions and offer their own suggestions for improvement. Collaboration is key when outsourcing, and Branson knows this better than anyone.

His final rules stresses the need for you to keep the lines of communication open with everyone on your team. You don't just outsource and then disappear. You need to stay connected and in tune with what's going on. If you're not approachable, or if you don't make it known to everyone that you are in fact approachable, you're likely to lose connection with not only the people on your team but also what's going on in your business. Obviously that's not a recipe for success. If you're not connected and in touch with what's happening, you'll be in a poor position to identify early warning signs of problems that might be occurring. Putting out full-blown fires is a lot more difficult than tamping out a little flame. So as the person who's outsourcing, you need to reaffirm to everyone at the start and consistently thereafter that you are always available to hear not only good things but also issues and challenges that are occurring. Ultimately, if you're connected to your team, they're far more likely to also be connected to each other. It's that kind of cohesion that leads to success in the long term.

As you're starting to plan out how you will be outsourcing, keep all of these examples in mind. Needing other people isn't a bad thing. It's necessary for becoming who you want to be and achieving all that you want in this life—your life.

BEGINNING WHERE WE STARTED: THE POWER OF REFLECTION

You now have read the entire Life Ledger process—and hopefully you are in the midst of experiencing its benefits by transforming your life to achieve all the goals and success you've desired. But a core aspect of this—and something that's built into every aspect of the Life Ledger—is the importance of reflection.

Life is full of fits and bursts. We can all look back at various times in our lives when we were depressed or full of energy and passion. There are invariably times when you're happy and other times you're sad. In many ways, life is in fact a rollercoaster—it can be thrilling at times, but also downright frightening; and as we come to the end of a particularly thrilling ride, we have the sense of peace and calm, and maybe (depending on how crazy the roller coaster was) a sense of accomplishment. This is all to say that these kinds of emotional changes always end—even the ones we want to continue forever.

But here's the thing, the secret people don't typically discover until it's often too late. If you want the good rides to last forever, you have to keep them going yourself. It's not easy, and it's not done in one genius move or another. Rather, it's accomplished incrementally, in the small things you do, each and every day.

The secret to keeping focused, whether in the midst of a horrible stretch of your ride or one of the best, is to constantly engage in reflection. The ability to reflect is not only what makes us human, it's what sustains us, what keeps us going, and what, ultimately, allows us to enduringly thrive.

I haven't been discussing this aspect of reflection throughout because I don't have to; it's built into everything that I've told you to do, starting with the Life Ledger itself. The daily ritual of writing your goals in the Life Ledger twice a day, every day, is a practice in self-reflection. It forces you to think about what you want, which helps you to determine if you still want it. When you begin a certain goal, a certain ride, for example, you're all in—of course you want to do it! That's why you wrote it down in the first place! But, as we all know, any ride—even the most exciting at first—can get boring after a while. It can start to feel routine. Once you know all the angles, once you're familiar with the biggest dips and highest climbs, it can become something you "just do" without even knowing why. That's when you fall into operating mode.

But if you're reflecting every day by writing down your goals in the Life Ledger, you've greatly reduced the risk of this happening. Why? Because you'll be acutely aware of any ebb in your enthusiasm. You'll start to know on a daily basis (not after months or even years) if your goal has lost its luster. Maybe it's because you've already accomplished it and you hadn't actually realized it. Maybe it's because on your journey, new opportunities or new ventures have become more interesting to you. Whatever the case may be, you'll be attuned to these shifts and changes in your attitude and motivation because of your incremental ability to reflect through the Life Ledger.

In all my time doing the Life Ledger, there's only been one goal that I've had continuously from the very beginning: You will not have a drink today. It's the one goal that I've never revised or changed or removed altogether because, as a recovering alcoholic, I can't. I have to reaffirm this goal to myself each and every day. I have to take the time to reflect on why I can't have a drink and also reflect on all of the positives that have come from me not having a drink on one day, as well as the compounding positives of not having a drink on two consecutive days, and then two consecutive weeks, and then two consecutive months, and then two consecutive years.

What was once merely an opportunity for drinking and, in a very real sense, losing myself, has, through not drinking, through being sober every single day, become an opportunity for growth and personal enrichment. For example, weekends for me used to just involve planning on when I was going to drink and where I was going to drink. The same would go for any trips I took too. Trips, even business trips, were a liability for me. Going to conferences or traveling, that became a liability. Now when I go on trips, every trip I go on—business or leisure—is for personal growth. I'm going to improve myself, and that's an asset. Before, I was going to not improve myself. I was going to get away from reality. That was the reason that I went.

And even the simplest things I derive more pleasure from now. I enjoy food more. I enjoy the people that I meet. I actually remember the people that I meet. I enjoy the atmosphere of the restaurant or the atmosphere of the club or whatever it is. Alcohol for me was deadening a lot of my senses that I didn't realize. I doubt that I really even understood the real taste of food for a long period of time. I'm saying most of my adult life, I don't think I really, really ever enjoyed food, which is crazy.

But none of this would be possible without daily reflection. I patted myself on the back so many times— potential "mission accomplished" moments. And those are the moments when, if you're not careful, you get complacent, you feel like you've "reached your goal." But for me, with this goal, I'll never "reach" it. I can't afford to let my guard down. I have to continually reflect on where I was and where I am now because, even to this day, I say no to alcohol at least two or three times a day. To have the strength to do that requires an inordinate amount of daily conviction, which can only be achieved through daily reflection.

So the Life Ledger makes this type of reflection a fundamental aspect of your daily existence. But so do the other elements of the five pillars—the rest of your Creation Foundation.

The very act of beating the sun up allows you space at the start of every day for reflection. The trick here is that by beating the sun up, you're also beating 99 percent of the population up. The world is sleeping while you're awake. That kind of solitude, whether you are consciously trying or not, allows for reflection. Of course, this won't always be the case—sometimes you're just thinking about what you watched on TV last night or something completely inane. But having that space to yourself every day will allow you to think and reflect in ways you wouldn't otherwise be able to.

Obviously morning meditation is a very conscious, intentional form of reflection. There's no real surprise here. As I said, it's an incredible and profoundly powerful way to center yourself and maintain a sense of who you are, where you belong, and what you want in life— in the short term as well as the long term. Morning Meditation helps you stay focused not only on what's important in your life, but also what's important in life generally. This is vital to building the discipline and focus to reach your goals.

Exercising, for me, is also a time for reflection. I actually didn't intend for this to be—it kind of just happened this way. When I was younger and would exercise, I'd have my headphones in, cranking Guns N' Roses or whatever music would psych me up for my workout. And when I started exercising regularly again, I reverted back to what I did as a kid—especially when I would run (which I hate doing). But one day, my phone died when I was in the middle of a run, and I had to do the last half with no music to distract me. It was one of those surprise lightbulb moments. With no music blaring in my ear, I could, for the first time, hear the birds while I was running. I could hear kids playing in a backyard. I could hear the sound of a distant lawnmower. More than anything else, I could hear me. I could hear myself breathing. I could hear each breath I took, and I know it might sound really weird, but it was exhilarating. It made me, in a really weird and unexpected way, aware of myself. I never used music again when I ran, or for any exercise. Now I just let my mind wander when I'm working out. Sometimes I think about nothing. Sometimes I think about stupid stuff. But sometimes I do find myself reflecting—on recent days, or weeks, or, sometimes, life.

Finally, brain training provides the need for reflection, albeit in an indirect way. Clearly the purpose of brain training is not necessarily for reflection, not for turning inward, but instead for turning outward—for expanding your horizons, building your knowledge and curiosity. But the act of always having to choose ways to train your brain means you also have to be reflecting on what you want to train your brain to do. Certainly, you don't want to take the time to train your brain to do things that have no relevance or meaning in your life, that won't get you closer to achieving what you want in life. So in order to select constructive activities to brain train, you also have to be continuously mindful of your goals, of who you are and what you want. So the activities you choose for brain training indirectly require constant reflection.

All of these opportunities built into the Life Ledger process will help ensure your resilience in achieving all that you want and reaching your full potential not just for now, not just over the next six months or a year, or even two years, but for your entire life. As your circumstances change, you get older and meet new people and develop new relationships, your constant reflection practices will ensure that you revise and adjust your priorities as you go. In this way, you'll be ready to meet any challenge, overcome any obstacle—and you'll do so with a love life and a passion for living that you never thought possible.

CHAPTER 9

The Four Foundations of Wealth Creation

IF YOU'VE GOTTEN TO THIS point, you've worked your way through the Life Ledger process. Everyone's goals are different. For some, it's wanting to be a better parent, for others it's about being a better boyfriend, girlfriend, husband, or wife. Some people who do the Daily Ledger are trying to be more philanthropic and do more community service to help those in need. Some people might be trying to change jobs, while others want to change their entire career. Some people will want to expand an existing business, while still others may want to start a business for the very first time. We're all different, and we all come to the Life Ledger with different experiences and expectations. The good news is that the Life Ledger is a lifelong process of learning, growing, and achieving all that you want in life. Committing to the Life Ledger is transformative and will enrich your life forever!

I separate out this chapter from the core steps of the Life Ledger, however, because this chapter is specifically focused on wealth creation, which may not relate to everyone's goals who is doing the Life Ledger. It's not to say you still can't benefit from this chapter—I think everyone can! I just want to make sure you understand the focus going in and why it's set apart from the essential steps I just laid out for doing the Life Ledger. That all said, I hope you do keep reading, because following these steps has helped immensely in scaling my businesses and increasing my wealth. It can do the same for you.

As I've said throughout this book, accounting is the language of business. That is what I was told growing up in a house full of CPAs. However, after working in this industry for nearly two decades and owning my own firm for more than a decade, I have come to the conclusion that it's more than just a language. No doubt does a financial statement or tax return tell a story of your business over a period of time. But it does not provide you with the steps to take to develop true wealth, lasting wealth, that can help provide a level of security for you and those that you love and care for.

These are uncertain times for so many people. Just in the past fifteen years, we've seen a housing market crash that destroyed the lives and dreams of so many people. Then we've faced an unprecedented pandemic, which put millions of people out of their jobs, upended entire industries, and transformed the nature of work possibly forever. And if that wasn't enough, now we're facing inflation escalating at rates unseen in decades that diminishes the value of every dollar hardworking people earn, and the price of housing continues to rise in ways very much reminiscent of the housing crash over a decade ago that set off the Great Recession. Like so many others, you might be asking yourself any number of questions related to your savings and long-term financial security: How do I develop true wealth? How can I make more money? How do I protect what I have made? How do I multiply my money? How do I create passive income? When is the right time for me to invest?

I get these questions all the time, and I have come up with many answers over the years tailored to the needs of my individual clients because it really so often depends on your current situation. It also depends on your definition of wealth, which can and does differ from person to person. For some people, having just enough money to live on and be happy would allow them to feel wealthy. For others, wealth might have a number value, such as earning six figures a year, or having $1 million in savings, or owning a business valued at $50 million. For still other people, being wealthy might not have to do with financial assets at all. Your situation and definition of wealth will shape the types of goals that you set and the types of plans you pursue.

But over the years, as I have answered hundreds of questions from clients to help them find and navigate their path to wealth, I began to see some similarities that were foundational to everyone's individual journeys. I began to discern basic principles that could be applied to everyone's individual situations.

I have reviewed thousands of tax returns and financial statements, and our team has consulted with more than 10,000 clients who own businesses and have created massive amounts of income. I began to notice certain trends and strategies that were used consistently and religiously. I observed how they carried themselves on a daily basis, how they protected their income, and how they planned. They saved to invest in a diligent and strategic way, they invested in passive income, achieved success in a more rapid and consistent fashion than most others, and they always planned for taxes. They accounted for every cent that they earned but were also generous at the same time. They seem to be fulfilled, and they all had a purpose. After these many client interactions and experiences, I was able to distill all that I learned into a process that I think anyone can follow.

There are four foundations to wealth creation, and this is what I want to introduce to you. These are simple steps, and they work. You just have to learn about them yourself and then execute. Before we get into the four steps, you have to define what wealth means to you. So we'll start with what I call the Wealth Blueprint.

THE WEALTH BLUEPRINT

If financial wealth building is one of your Life Ledger goals, you may already be more than a couple of steps into figuring out your Wealth Blueprint. But let's take a step back from that for a second, so you can reflect a bit more and perhaps a bit deeper about the very idea of wealth and what it means in your life.

First, let's play a word association game: open up a blank Word document or grab a piece of paper and a pen. I'm going to say a word and as soon as you see the word, I want you to just start writing the first thoughts and ideas that come to mind. Don't inhibit yourself—there isn't a right or wrong answer. Just be open and honest about what thoughts and feelings this word elicits from you when you hear it. Ready? What do you think about when you think about the word *wealth*?

Okay, now give yourself a brain break because I'm going to ask you one more question, and I want you to answer in the same way as you did before—that is, I'm going to give you a word and you just have to respond immediately about what comes to mind without thinking about it. Again, there are no right or wrong answers here. Just be honest with your immediate thoughts and response. Ready? What do you think about when you think about *happiness*?

Now, as you look at both your responses, you need to evaluate how closely they align in terms of your financial goals. That is, are the things that you think about in relation to happiness going to require what you think about when you think about wealth? Does your happiness depend on a certain level of wealth? And if so, what level would be sufficient?

I ask this not to complicate your life or to try to confuse you. I'm asking because sometimes we default to certain ideas about wealth. We might automatically think about having a huge mansion with vast green manicured lawns and gardens and people who attend to our every need. Or we might think of fancy cars or traveling the world. But happiness is a bit more personalized; it's based on feelings we've experienced at various times in our lives since we were kids. Even if you had a rough childhood, you can remember moments that you were happy—truly happy—and those memories and that feeling stay with us over the course of our lives into adulthood. And then of course as adults we experience our happiness in different ways. We evolve. But what's important is how your ideas of happiness have evolved to align with your financial understanding of wealth. They shouldn't be vastly different. Each should work to enhance the other.

Once you've done some deeper thinking about this, you may discover that your understanding of wealth aligns with what you've already done with your Life Ledger, and that's great! No opportunity for self-reflection is ever wasted, so this exercise will just help to reaffirm and bolster your confidence in the goals you've already set for yourself.

But it's also possible that you discovered some gaps or some contradictions in doing this exercise, which now provides you with an opportunity to revise your thinking and your goals. Ultimately, the big question is this: What do you want? This, too, is a difficult question for many people to answer. So let's do it right now!

Again, grab your piece of paper or your tablet or laptop or whatever and write down everything you want. It can include anything and everything, this is not just materialistic items. It is everything. What do you want in your life? A beautiful family, money, homes, businesses, etc. It can be anything. Successful people who are creating wealth define what they want first in detail and leave nothing out. True wealth is getting what you want. No matter what it is. This will be your Wealth Blueprint. Remember, your work doing the Life Ledger is helpful here. To accomplish anything, you must write down something. So make your list right now and let's begin to break it down into actionable steps within my Wealth Creation system.

The thing about money is that it means nothing in and of itself. For the longest time, it was just images printed on paper. Now it's increasingly becoming just numbers on a digital screen. Always remember that money is merely a tool for getting what you actually want in life; that could be anything from a material good (like a car or nice clothes), to psychological calm (peace of mind or security), to a way of experiencing and doing what you want (ski trips, visiting family and friends, traveling to another country). It's essential to understand that this tool—money—needs to be used to get those things, whatever they may be. Following these four steps will help you get the money you need to attain what you want out of life.

The four steps are as follows:

1. Generating Monthly Income

2. Identifying Tax Savings

3. Protecting Your Income

4.   Investing in Yourself and Others

Let's explore each of these steps in detail.

Step 1: Generating Monthly Income

How much should I make a month? You are the only one who can answer this question. You must figure out how much income to generate in order to reach your goals and accomplish your own wealth creation. Generating monthly "free" cash flow is extremely important to executing your wealth plan. It's so important that it serves as the very first step you have to take. No matter who you are, generating adequate monthly income is core to anyone's Wealth Blueprint. Generating monthly income requires four essential components, many of which will be familiar to you already with your work doing the Life Ledger, but they're worth reviewing here again—that's how important this is to Wealth Creation.

1.   The Decision

2.   Goal Writing and Affirmations

3.   Accountability

The Decision

Nothing happens until you make a decision. It doesn't matter what the decision is, good or bad. When you are ready to start generating monthly income that is going to be sustainable and allows you to execute your Wealth Blueprint, you must make a decision to do so. This first component is pretty simple, but it's not easy to do and nothing will happen until you take this step. It's not easy for this reason: too many people go back and forth on what they want.

If you executed the exercises in making your Wealth Blueprint, then you're ahead of the game and will be less likely to flip flop or be uncertain about what it is that you want. The blueprint will definitely help you make a decision to move toward your goals. Once a decision is made, you can move forward with using the second component. But like everything we've talked about in this entire book, you need to write it down! You need to declare it to yourself and the world!

Literally write the following down: "I am laying the foundation of my wealth system. I made the decision to increase my wealth and finally get what I want. I have made the decision today and will do whatever it takes to increase my wealth in a systematic way moving forward in my life."

Goal Writing and Affirmations

All of my mentors and business coaches say the same thing when it comes to goal writing. They all believe it is essential to increasing your wealth and generating your desired monthly income level. We've done this throughout the Life Ledger, but if your Life Ledger goals weren't necessarily about finances and wealth, you need to apply those same practices here. If they were about finances and wealth, then you need to reaffirm those goals here as you build your Wealth Creation plan. Everything stems from writing down your goals every day. Just as with your Life Ledger, you need to write your goals down twice a day or at any time during the day when you start to feel fear and doubt creep in.

Goal writing is the standard operating procedure for your life and your business. It is the standard to hold yourself to and will completely change your life if you submit to this simple fact. Goal writing will get you what you want. It is a simple process and takes less than five minutes each time you do it. I don't know about you, but I will commit ten minutes every day to achieving my wealth list. The most common objection I receive from clients when I discuss this second component to this foundation is that they do not know what goals to write down. Let me help you overcome this objection right now once and for all. It is not about the goals that you are writing down. It is about the fact that you are following a system to put you in a mindset to achieve the goals. If you do not know what goals to write down, then write down "Determine my goals" twice a day. This will create discipline and consistency in your daily routine, which is essential to reaching your goals.

Make sure when you are writing these goals you write them as they are happening. Below are some examples of goals:

- I want to make more than $1 million per year.

- I want my net worth to be more than $500 million.

- I want to own a beautiful home in St. Lucia.

- I want to own an island.

- I want to be one of the largest donors to charities around the world.

- I want to create a new community center in my town.

- I want to own companies that I am able to control from a distance and have great people who work for me every day.

- I want a career that will earn me $100,000.

- I want to own $1 billion in real estate properties across the globe.

These are some examples of some financial wealth creation goals to give you an idea. If you are already writing your financial goals down twice a day, every day, per your Life Ledger, that is incredible. Keep doing it. If you are not, then figure out your financial goals right now and start this practice immediately, as in today.

Remember there are zero excuses for this not to happen if you are serious about your financial goals. This will remind you of why you are doing what you are doing every day and provide you with the confidence to accomplish and overcome any fear and doubt that might come into your mind over time.

To go along with your financial goal writing, another simple process at least once a day is to write down your affirmations. Affirmation in the dictionary is defined as a short sentence that motivates, inspires, and encourages you to take action and realize your goals. In other words, write down uplifting, positive statements. These declarations can help you to challenge yourself and also help overcome any negative, self-sabotaging thoughts. My business coach helped me to be aware and implement this into my daily routine, and I assure you they work. Affirmations are a powerful way to improve your mindset on a daily basis. Research has shown that they can increase our feelings of self-worth.

Let's face it, if you are like me, you are your own worst critic. It's time to change the game and affirm yourself each day. It is so much easier to affirm others, but you must remain consistent and disciplined and affirm yourself each day to get what you want. Become your biggest cheerleader, affirm yourself daily, and write it down. Here are some affirmations to take from or inspire you to come up with your own:

- I am confident in my ability to generate wealth as it is defined by me.

- I give myself space to learn and grow.

- I allow myself to be who I am without judgment.

- I give myself care and attention that I deserve.

- My drive and ambition allow me to achieve my goals.

- I am good at helping others achieve their goals.

- I trust that I am on the right path.

- My mind is full of brilliant ideas.

- I am learning valuable lessons from myself every day.

- I am at peace with who I am as a person.

Goal writing and affirmations are important components to generating monthly income for a few reasons. Most importantly, goal writing and affirmations instill consistency and discipline into your daily life. The wealthiest individuals I know all have consistency and discipline in their lives, and this is a system to follow to develop those skills, as we do with the Life Ledger.

Accountability

Accountability is the third and final component in the first foundation of wealth creation in generating monthly income. Accountability is the "time" it takes to achieve your goal. Accountability works similarly to how it does in the general Life Ledger:

1. Write it down with I statements, and/or

2. Share your goals with someone you trust—an Accountability Partner of sorts, but only for your financial goals. This is the person who you will check in with, or who will check in on you, to see how you're holding to and actively working on your goals.

Both of these are effective and will force you to act when you need to. In order to generate the amount of monthly income you want, you need to achieve your goals. The fastest way to cure that foundation is through accountability. We do not like accountability. As I told you earlier in the book, I hated it for the longest time, and it cost me so much that I almost lost everything. But you'll be amazed at how much more and faster you will accomplish your financial goals if you make yourself accountable to yourself and to others. You can literally shrink time with accountability.

I encourage you to do employ both strategies. Write down your goals and share with your trusted person (your Financial Accountability Partner) everything from this first foundation. Ask them to follow up with you on your goals and execution. Trust me, it will help keep you on track and get you achieving more and faster—which is the point.

Step 2: Identifying Tax Savings

Your goals and what amount of monthly income you are generating determines how you are going to save money on taxes in the future. I encourage all entrepreneurs and business owners who generate more than $100,000 per year in revenue to look very closely at their taxes. It's imperative that you are executing tax savings strategies each year for one simple reason: outside of your mortgage, the amount you spend on taxes is very likely your biggest annual expense.

Clients who execute tax savings strategies are far more likely to keep more of the money they are generating on a monthly basis and, therefore, create more future wealth because they have more money to invest in other assets, as well as in themselves.

And let me be clear, this tax savings is not only meant to increase your monthly income moving forward but also create passive income in the future. This foundation is so important, I dedicate the entire final chapter of this book to discussing strategies for tax savings, which will provide you with increasingly greater wealth accumulation.

The two most critical components are generating monthly income and then identifying tax strategies. Once those are executed and continued moving forward, they provide the fundamentals needed to execute the final two foundations of wealth creation.

Step 3: Protecting Your Income

In this third foundation of wealth creation, we begin to multiply our efforts through utilizing life insurance. Now some of you may be reading this and saying, "Oh, great, another life insurance guy!" But remember, I'm a CPA. I gain nothing from "selling you insurance." I'm laying this out as a foundation for wealth creation because, well, it is. I have recommended these strategies to create wealth my whole career and use them all myself, and I see how it increases the value and wealth of my clients.

Anything I promote or advocate for, I absolutely do myself, and each one of these steps I am performing every day, month, and year. In short, they work, that's why I do them. Life insurance is what wealthy individuals use to protect their income streams in case they die, and it also provides incredible retirement benefits and creates tax-free wealth for the future.

But let me be clear here, this foundation of wealth creation requires an enormous amount of discipline and patience and an overall understanding of taxes and how they will work in the future. That's why this foundation necessarily builds off the second foundation. You can't fully understand and utilize life insurance to your greatest advantage if you don't fully understand your tax situation.

On top of that, most individuals do not realize that life insurance has more valuable benefits while you are alive than if you are dead. So let me lay out the five reasons why life insurance is so important to wealth creation:

1. Disciplined savings plan—It requires you to save a certain monthly amount every month, quarter, or year. This provides you a way to

practice saving money for the future in a vehicle that will continue to grow in value tax free.

2. Death Benefit—On a permanent or term life insurance policy, you always have a death benefit. The way I like to describe this is it protects the future income that you have if, unfortunately, you pass away. Your loved ones will have the money required to take care of all their living expenses if set up correctly.

3. Personal Financial Statement—You are able to claim the cash value in the life insurance policy as a part of your net worth when reporting for your personal financial statement.

4. Your Own Bank—When you begin to create cash value in the policy, you have the ability to borrow against that cash value for short-term or long-term cash needs. It's a very low interest rate and you can borrow the money within a two-day period.

5. Tax-Free Wealth—The cash value of the policy grows tax free and provides a way to take tax-free distributions upon reaching retirement age. If tax rates rise in the future, as they most likely will, this will enable you to take advantage of the tax-free wealth strategy even more

because you will fund the policy at a much lower tax rate than when you decide to take the money and distribute it out of the policy.

Most taxpayers who are in the $250,000 and higher income tax bracket will begin to utilize life insurance as an alternative retirement vehicle and take advantage of all five of these benefits immediately. Life insurance provides you the ability to confidently grow tax-free wealth over a longer period of time. It's difficult to overstate how important this is for wealth creation.

A simple way to realize the power of this foundation is to take two basic factors: one being your age, the other the amount of money that is disposable and that you can contribute to a life insurance fund. Then approach a few different life insurance companies or your accountant and see how much that money will grow by the time you reach retirement age, which, by the way, also depends on your personal situation and when you want to retire. For some people that might be fifty, for other people, they may never want to retire. We have a client, for example, who is thirty-two and took advantage of this strategy and is contributing $10,000 per month into a policy. Her contributions over time will create approximately $10 million of tax-free wealth when she retires.

Step 4: Investing in Yourself and Others

You might often hear the term "passive income" and how important it is for wealth creation. Don't get me wrong, it is, but in my mind, it is only a part of the fourth foundation of wealth creation. Let me explain why.

Wealthy individuals are those who are getting what they want, but they are getting what they want in large part because they are defining what they want. And they are defining what they want by adhering to the first three foundations. They are defining and setting their goals. They are generating income to meet those goals. They are continually seeking ways of minimizing their tax expenses. And they are protecting their long-term income through insurance. True passive income is not achievable without the application of these foundations.

Passive income is also not achievable without having an incredible group of people working with you on a daily basis. Ironically, true passive income requires a ton of active participation over a long period of time not only from you but from those trusted others around you. As I explained earlier in the book, no one is truly self-made. We need other people to achieve the success that we want in life. It's not different for your financial goals. In fact, it might be most important to achieving your financial goals.

As I was thinking about these four foundations, I discovered that "investing in real estate" and other "passive investments" isn't what the ultrawealthy did or even what the moderately wealthy did. They instead continued to improve themselves and continued to do what got them to a place of wealth in the first place. The truly wealthy discovered and kept discovering that what they truly wanted continued to change over the years as they changed, as we discuss in the Life Ledger process.

Once you've established and execute the first three foundations of wealth creation, you need to remember to invest in yourself and others. You come first, of course. Invest in yourself above all else. As we've discussed all along in this book, it all starts with you. And that's not a bad or selfish thing. It's like the emergency directions that you hear before your plane takes off. If a problem arises in flight, and the oxygen masks drop from the ceiling, you're supposed to first secure the mask for yourself before helping others. Why? Because you'll be of no help to anyone if you pass out due to oxygen deprivation! However, once you're secure and stabilized, you can start helping everyone around you as well. It's the same in your real life. Investing in yourself first will ensure that you are stable and secure enough to start helping and investing in those around you.

So be sure to execute simple, ongoing plans for self-improvement. Expand your network, schedule a trip, go to a conference, take time for self-care by investing in a business coach, a therapist, etc. Continue to work on you and improve you, because this whole idea of creating wealth truly begins and ends with you.

Continue to invest in your business. If you have a business, invest back into it before investing in anything else and after you are sure to invest in yourself. Investing in your business will help to create culture, improve your team, increase efficiencies, and make it a stronger company every year. And, yes, also invest in passive activities. As I've said, no activity is truly passive. It all takes work one way or the other, or you have to pay someone to do the work or make the investment for you. You should only invest in passive income once you have $100,000 in your bank account that you do not need to invest in yourself or your business.

Finally, invest in others. This is how you begin to scale your business—by outsourcing responsibilities to others. This will allow them to learn, grow, and thrive along with you, which creates that magical self-nourishing feedback loop. You're stable and secure through taking the time to invest in yourself. You then are able to begin scaling and elevating and investing in those around you. The people around you begin to learn, grow, and thrive, which enhances your ability to cultivate and elevate yourself and your business. And so the cycle continues this way, as does your generation of wealth.

And though this is the last foundation, it's the foundation that allows you to begin to multiply and scale your ability to generate income exponentially, which, happily, brings us back to the first foundation of wealth creation. Investing in yourself first, then your business, and then others is the order in which you will be able to shrink time and scale yourself and others.

On a personal note, true wealth to me is my family, relationships, and my faith that I have been fortunate enough to continue to improve over the years. The money, assets, and other investments accumulated along the way are important to me, but only to the extent that they nourish my life, relationships, faith, and all those who I love and trust and help me to become the person I aspire to be. Ultimately, I want to create businesses that provide an incredible culture for others to achieve their personal, professional, and financial goals. After all, not everyone is a business owner, and I feel that it is my responsibility to create businesses that will help others feel fulfilled and create their wealth.

The ability for you to recognize what you want sooner rather than later is going to help you understand what success and wealth truly are to you. One of my favorite things to do is to work with a client that is confused and doesn't have a plan. I love to listen to their issues and create a system that will help them to understand what went wrong, if anything did, and how this system is going to bring them the solution they need to keep moving onward. That is what brings me the most joy and wealth, and I hope that this system will provide you with the foundation to truly build your own wealth in whatever way you define it.

CHAPTER 10

Five Pillars of Mastering Tax Strategy

So I CONCLUDE THE LIFE Ledger with this chapter not because it's the coolest and not because it will change your life—at least not in the way the Life Ledger will. Rather, I conclude with this discussion of tax strategy because it's so critical to fully executing the foundations of wealth creation. As I said last chapter, for most people, the biggest annual expenses are one's mortgage and…taxes. And though paying taxes might seem like a negligible variable if you're fortunate enough to be increasing your annual income, I can assure you there is a giant wealth (that gets even more giant over time) between those who master tax strategy and those who do not. The former will have many thousands, sometimes millions, more dollars at the finish line than the latter, even if their annual revenue is similar. So yes, tax planning is incredibly important to wealth creation. So let's get down to it.

Plan your work and work your plan is what my father always told me. I apply this to every client I've worked with. Every taxpayer needs a plan to follow with their taxes whether they are a W2 employee or a multi-entity entrepreneur. There are several parts of the tax code the average taxpayer does not take advantage of, and it's simply because they do not have a plan. They have no idea what they can utilize in the tax code. I'm going to take care of that for you right now by providing you with the five most effective strategies that affect almost every taxpayer at some time. These are proven strategies that will save you money every year on taxes and are easily utilized by entrepreneurs and small business owners.

I'm a big believer in being a practitioner, not a perfectionist. This is something I remind all of my clients. No plan is perfect; however, a solid plan can lead to consistency and predictability over time. Consistency and predictability are two very key ingredients in business. The more consistent and predictable your business is, the more successful it will be. This is what investors, banks, your team, and the IRS is looking for in your business. These five pillars are your new tax strategy plan.

PILLAR 1: TAX PLANNING

The most common belief clients have about tax planning is that they need to decide to purchase a vehicle or piece of equipment by the end of the year to save money on taxes. Most taxpayers think tax planning starts around September or October, maybe even December. It doesn't. The most successful business owners tax plan all year long. Every month, they make decisions around their cash flow and taxes. Taxes are the largest outflow of cash for a majority of businesses, yet many owners do not have a plan for the cash outflow. They don't know when it is going out the door, and they don't know how much is going out the door. The idea of tax planning is simple and again revolves around the key ingredients to a business: consistency and predictability.

Predicting your taxable income is possible. There are simple tools on the web that can easily help provide you with a decent estimate of your annual taxable income. Knowing your taxable income allows you to make better decisions about your investments and cash flow.

The IRS requires two different forms of payment filing taxes throughout the year. You either withhold your federal income tax payments on your paycheck each pay period or you pay quarterly estimated tax payments. Quarterly estimated tax payments are due on April 15, June 15, September 15, and January 15 of the following year. Did you realize that the IRS will charge you penalties and interest for not paying enough money during the year? This is called the safe harbor calculation. The IRS requires payment in 90 percent of your current year's tax amount or 110 percent of your prior year's tax amount on your tax return to avoid penalties and interest. This is why it is important to execute tax planning to avoid unnecessary penalties and interest.

The second payment of taxes is made after the tax return is complete. Based on the total tax that is due when filed, either money will be owed or a tax return will be issued. If you receive a fantastic refund, this means you paid too much tax. If you have to pay tax when you complete your return, that is okay! This means you did not pay enough money during the year and now it is time to pay up. The most common misconception for taxpayers is if money is owed, you do not need to pay it on April 15, you can extend your return. Yes, you may extend to FILE the return, but time cannot be extended to make the payment. When you extend the return, the tax payment is still due on

April 15. This is commonly misunderstood, and taxpayers typically miss this opportunity to save money on penalties and interest.

PILLAR 2: ENTITY STRUCTURE

An entity is an organization created by one or more individuals to carry out the functions of a business, and that maintains a separate legal existence for tax purposes. It can be created at the local or state level. The IRS provides a federal identification number to entities, but the type of entity is technically decided at the state level with the department of revenue. Entities refer to the structure of the business more than what the business does. Six different entity types are most popular among business owners:

- sole proprietorship
- general partnerships
- limited liability companies
- limited partnerships
- S corporations
- corporations

The economic entity assumption is an accounting principle that distinguishes the transactions inside a business from that of its owner. Each business unit or division maintains its books and accounting records, specific to the business operations. This is important in utilizing this pillar because you must maintain the separation of the business activity and the individual activity. This creates a very clear line between business and personal expenses, which is critical to utilizing this strategy.

The easiest entity to form is a sole proprietorship. You only need an idea and your social security number to start this kind of entity. This type of entity does not offer any tax benefits other than it opens up the opportunity to write off more deductions against your W2 income or 1099 income.

There is zero liability protection with this type of entity, and you are not required to file any forms with the state to form the entity. The activity in this entity is recorded on your Schedule C on your individual income tax return. It is critical to creating a business plan that includes your skills, experience, and education, as it relates to what the business does. This will provide additional support to ensure that you are taking advantage of every tax deduction you can to reduce your taxable income. This is the easiest way to take advantage of this pillar of entity structure.

General partnerships are the next-easiest entity to form utilizing the IRS website. I recommend consulting with an attorney when forming a general partnership or any of the following entities. A general partnership does not require you to have any type of written agreement, but it is a good practice to have any partnership agreement or verbal agreement in writing, but it can also be documented on a napkin—literally! Any partnership from a general partnership to an LLC can be documented this simply; however, it is not advisable. There are specific rules and revenue procedures that favor these "small general partnerships."

Limited liability companies are a more formal version of a general partnership, and they provide limited liability to the members of the entity. Unlike a sole proprietorship and even a general partnership, there is no liability to the owner of an LLC. LLCs definitely should be created by a professional firm, such as an accounting firm or a law firm. I see these types of entities formed daily the wrong way and members of the entity believe they are protected, but they are not because it was formed incorrectly. An LLC must file articles of organization with the secretary of state that is providing the limited liability.

Most taxpayers fail to understand that entity liability protection comes from the state in which the entity is formed, not the IRS or the federal government. There is not a lot of tax law around general partnerships or LLCs that provides more advantages to utilize this type of entity for income tax purposes. LLCs provide a variety of ways to allocate income, expenses, multiple ownership structures, and an overall variety of ways to recognize income among partners. I typically recommend this type of entity as a sole owner, which is called a Single Member Limited Liability Company (SMLLC), when you are first starting your business because it is simple, easy, and still provides limited liability, unlike a sole proprietorship.

Limited partnerships are most commonly used for real estate entities. A limited partnership has two types of partners: general and limited. A general partner is subject to all the liability in this type of partnership. The limited partners (LP) are subject to limited liability. These are typically utilized when the LP owns a piece of real estate and there is debt involved that some partners do not want to be "on the hook" for, so they are allowed limited liability in this type of setup. An additional benefit to the limited partners is they only receive passive income from the entity rather than active income, so it's received at a lesser tax rate than the general partner. At the same time, their losses are limited to only passive losses, unlike a general partner who would be able to take losses against any of their other active income. This is very complicated tax jargon, but it is the truth.

This sophisticated entity structuring has many nuances to it and should not be considered lightly when deciding to form this type of entity. You should always consult with a professional before executing any entity set up as there can be severe tax implications in the future if it is not handled correctly.

S corporations are my second favorite entity to form or convert other entities into. Typically, I do not recommend business owners to form S corps first because of the requirements to run an S corp, and they can be a risk compliance nightmare while trying to start a business. However, S corps provide a variety of important tax relief. The best time to form an S corp is when net income from your business is at least more than $250,000 per year. There is no advantage unless that is the case. The costs and additional items to comply with forming an S corp are prohibitive if that's not the baseline income for the entity.

To begin, you must pay yourself a W2 salary out of the S corp. This requires additional time, money, and energy to get set up. It must be a "reasonable salary" according to the IRS, and states have other rules around S corps, which may also not be to your advantage depending on the state. S corp entities, such as SMLLCs and LLCs, can elect to be taxed as an S corp by filing a Form 2553. This is typically done by a professional, but you can do it yourself if you choose; however,

I wouldn't take the risk. This is a strategy that allows you to maintain your LLC as an entity but provides you with the tax advantages of an S corp, which allows you to save more money in taxes utilizing corporate policies and the way you pay yourself. You can save so much money in taxes by establishing these corporate policies, but they must be in writing and they must be followed. The S corp allows for more formal corporate policies to be in place, unlike the partnership entity options. This is why I believe the S corp is the most versatile and tax-payer-friendly entity out of all of them.

Finally, corporations are the last type of entity we will review. The main item you need to know about corporations is that they do not mean you are going to pay less in taxes just because they have a lower tax rate. Right now, the rate is 21 percent, which is very low, but most do not realize that when you have a corporation you will run into "double taxation." You will be taxed at the corporate level and the individual level on the same money. This is the opposite of flow-through entities like partnerships and S corps that only tax the taxpayer on one level. The complicated structure and double taxation are why I rarely recommend traditional corporate entities.

PILLAR 3: TAX METHOD OF ACCOUNTING

Every time I review a tax return of a business or individual I always want to make sure I understand the story the return is telling me. A tax return, to the common taxpayer, is a bunch of complicated forms with lots of numbers, questions, statements, and checkboxes to complete that seem to mean very little. When I review a return, I see a story about who my client is and what my client does.

The third pillar of mastering tax strategy is the tax method of accounting, and it will help you understand the story in tax returns. When I review a return, I'm always looking for a number of different things: the income of the taxpayer, what status they are filing under, the number of dependents and why they are dependents, the taxpayer's occupation, and what industry the taxpayer is in if it is a business. Different industries have different ways of reporting income and, according to the taxpayer's occupation, provide certain skills, experience, and education. This variance in industry and experience will allow you to decide on a method of accounting to report income and expenses. There are a few different methods of accounting. The industry determines the different types that may be used.

The most common tax methods of accounting are the accrual and cash methods. The accrual method allows you to recognize revenue and expenses on a more expedited basis, which can be good and bad for the taxpayer from a standpoint of paying tax. This is a more sophisticated method of reporting income and expenses and is not usually understood by the common taxpayer. The cash method of accounting is the most commonly used and can only be used as long as the business has less than twenty-five million in revenue or less.

Almost every individual reports their taxes on the cash method, but businesses are allowed to choose one or the other and can sometimes utilize a hybrid method between the two. This hybrid method requires a systematic way of documenting the strategies used. It can be a very effective method for tax savings, but I would not advise you to try this on your own. As I said earlier, the IRS is looking for consistency and predictability. The tax method of accounting has to be consistent and predictable and you cannot switch from one to the other from year to year. You must pick one and must be consistent when applying a tax method to your income and expense reporting.

There are other tax methods of accounting such as cash completed contract, accrual completed contract, hybrid, percentage completion, etc., but all of these methods are specific to certain businesses and industries; the main item is how they report their income and expenses. The revenue recognition policy of a business is determined by these tax methods of accounting and could be the difference between paying thousands in taxes one year and not paying anything. This is why it is such an important pillar and will change your outlook on your tax return preparation the more you investigate and learn about it.

PILLAR 4: SPECIALTY INDUSTRY: TAX CREDITS AND DEDUCTIONS

This pillar of mastering tax strategy is extremely beneficial to the right taxpayer, especially depending on their specific industry. Each business has specific industry tax credits and deductions that can be applied, and the only way to identify them is to know them and understand how they are applied.

Obscurity is the biggest obstacle to overcome in business, because people will not do business with you if they do not know what your business does or know how it can help them solve problems. Obscurity is also the biggest obstacle in taxes because the majority of taxpayers have no idea what parts of the tax code apply to their business. As the old saying goes, you don't know what you don't know, so in a specific industry, you could have competitors that are taking advantage of certain tax breaks and certain credits that you simply do not know about. Competitors using industry-specific tax breaks are saving money every year, which then affords them additional annual cash flow they can use to reinvest in their business and generate even more revenue. They could, for example, use that additional capital to advertise more, which would decrease their obscurity, potentially taking away more market share from you.

So you see, what seems like one simple omission in your tax strategy—not knowing all the tax breaks and deductions specific to an industry—actually means so much more and can, over time, have a profound impact on your business and your overall success and wealth. This is why tax planning is so important for business owners. It can change your cash flow by 20 percent to 30 percent each year, which can change your life.

Research and development (R&D) tax credits are the most overlooked tax credit for many industries. These credits don't mean that you have to be inventing something or developing new medical breakthroughs. R&D tax credits are available to almost any business that is making a product or process from beginning to end. The common misconception is you must be creating something brand new. That's not true. You have to be improving on the process and that's it. This credit is created by the people and wages that are involved in the creation of a new process, not the actual dollars invested in new equipment or energy-saving techniques. It is calculated by taking 6 percent of the total wages involved in the R&D activity.

Remember, a tax credit is a direct reduction of your tax; it is not a tax deduction. It creates way more value, and if you do not use the credit, it will roll forward against your future tax liability for fifteen years. These are very valuable credits and need to be taken advantage of as soon as possible in your business.

Cost segregation studies are a very unique tax strategy that allows you to accelerate the depreciation of a real estate purchase, in particular a twenty-seven-and-a-half- or thirty-nine-year piece of property. Commercial buildings purchased during the year typically have a thirty-nine-year life for depreciation purposes. This means the asset is written off over thirty-nine years evenly. A cost segregation study allows you to break that purchase up into a five-, seven-, or fifteen-year property. This allows the taxpayer to depreciate the property over a shorter period, which accelerates the depreciation utilizing section 179—depreciation or bonus depreciation. This is extremely powerful and is very useful for taxpayers in the real estate industry, particularly those who elect to buy and hold real estate for typically more than seven to ten years. It does not make sense to accelerate depreciation if you are planning to flip the property in a shorter timeframe. Unlike tax credits, these are deductions, so they do not pack as much initial punch as an R&D tax credit, but are still extremely beneficial when planning for taxes. They will result in a decreased tax liability and provide you more capital to deploy into your next big real estate deal!

Conservation easements are another specialty industry tax deduction. This is not as much a tax deduction related to a specific industry as it is related to a certain high-income taxpayer. Conservation easements are known as listed transactions with the IRS, which means they come under more scrutiny than most tax strategies. We have seen evidence of this in recent years because of the increased audit/examination activity involved with this tax deduction.

So why in the world would I discuss that in this chapter? Because, once again, you don't know what you don't know. Just because a specific strategy is under scrutiny does not mean that it is not a valid transaction. Scrutinizing tax returns is the IRS's job, after all. In section 170 of the tax code, the IRS allows you to write off the appraised value of a piece of property if you decide to contribute it to a conservation easement. This is the government's way of conserving the environment in a much less expensive way than creating a national or state park.

When you purchase a piece of property, you have three choices: develop it, buy and hold it as an investment, or contribute it to a conservation easement and decide to never develop it for eternity. When you decide on option three, the IRS requires you to do everything you would normally do to develop it up to the point in which you start to "dig dirt." Once you get to that point, you can elect to contribute the property to a land trust for the appraised value based on the possible development. This is recorded as an itemized deduction on Schedule A of your tax return and you can deduct up to 60 percent of your adjusted gross income utilizing this tax deduction. It is extremely powerful but requires several specialists and it's not an inexpensive deduction. For taxpayers with an AGI of $250,000 or more, it is a very powerful tax-planning tool in the tax code. The IRS has this categorized as a listed transaction because of rampant abuse relative to the valuations/appraisals used for this deduction. This is why it is important to partner with a CPA who uses specialists to help execute this strategy for their clients.

There are many other specialty industry tax credits and deductions that may apply to your business. The best way to assess any of them is to utilize tax planning so a professional can help you diagnose the credits and deductions that will help you save the most money on taxes. This will ensure you are utilizing every part of the tax code you can. Then you execute that plan year over year to minimize tax liability as your business continues to grow and evolve.

PILLAR 5: CAPTIVE INSURANCE COMPANIES

The fifth pillar of mastering tax strategy is captive insurance companies. This strategy is not used by a majority of taxpayers, but it can be a valuable strategy if employed effectively. It is a part of the five pillars because it is a strategy almost every business owner should aspire to utilize at some point in the life of their business. This strategy allows utilization of tax savings to invest into real estate, other markets, other businesses, and provides the opportunity to keep the money saved on taxes and transform the tax rate in which you report those taxes. This strategy utilizes a combination of the previous four pillars and is the culmination of all tax strategies.

A captive insurance company is your own insurance company. This pillar is reserved and only makes sense for taxpayers who make an excess of $500,000 of net income in their business, and they must have a use for insurance in their business. A captive insurance company is used to ensure different parts of your business from typical normal business insurance purposes to some specialty insurance purposes that you might be able to create in your business.

When you have your own insurance company, you will pay insurance premiums to that company and be able to recognize that expense and create a deduction in your operating business at a top rate of 37 percent. Inside the insurance company, this money is not recognized as income but as a reserve. The IRS allows you to reserve up to $2.5 million in insurance premium reserves. That means that you can defer $2.5 million in income from one year to the next. The captive insurance company can then invest this money inside the company. The insurance company is formed as a corporation and can pay dividends to the owners. So when insurance premiums have been invested and retained for at least a year, proceeds of those investments can be distributed at capital gains rates that are 20 percent to the owner of the corporation. So the power of a captive insurance company is it allows you to create a company in which you can convert money that is taxed at 37 percent into money that is taxed at 20 percent, up to $2.5 million. This would result in tax savings of approximately $425,000 every single year assuming you would utilize the maximum amount of the reserve.

Each time I describe this to clients, they say it's too good to be true; they hear it and decide that they don't want to pursue it, or they don't want to invest in what it takes to make it happen. It does take resources and time to make this happen, as it doesn't happen overnight. There is a monetary investment of approximately $25,000 to get a captive insurance company started and there is approximately $15,000 per year of maintenance costs, all of which is tax-deductible as well.

TAX SAVINGS STRATEGY: CONCLUDING THOUGHTS

As I stated at the beginning of this chapter, having a plan and working the plan is the most effective way to save money on taxes. The IRS is looking for a consistent and predictable tax strategy that is defendable and well within the IRS tax code. Business owners need to plan and execute the five pillars of mastering tax strategy to minimize their taxes on an annual basis; no matter the industry or the type of business, these strategies can be used for every single small business owner or taxpayer in America.

Tax Planning, entity structure, tax methods of accounting, specialty industry tax credits and deductions, and captive insurance companies are the five pillars of mastering tax strategy. These are the five ways you can minimize your tax bill every year and create that consistent, predictable plan. Pair these strategies with your Wealth Creation Foundation and your ongoing Life Ledger, and you are sure to continue growing your wealth as you transform your life. Good luck!

ABOUT THE AUTHOR

Photo credit: Emily Lester

JD FROST IS THE FOUNDER and CEO of CROFT & FROST, a firm that transcends traditional accounting and wealth creation. With both a CPA and his MBA, JD advises businesses on more than just their financials; he utilizes four foundations of wealth creation to help his clients, partners, and employees build courage and create wealth. As an entrepreneur, he knows what it takes to start—and scale—a business, and has used his years of experience in accounting to build a solid foundation for each and every one of his clients and businesses. JD and his partner, Paul Croft, share over thirty business ventures. They have helped clients and investors raise over $18 million and have closed $35 million in real estate and small business transactions in the past three years. Through entrepreneurship, sobriety, and fatherhood, JD has developed a ledger to become fully accountable to his life.